Appily

A Woman's Guide to Online Dating

Benjamin Daly

ISBN: 9781697332124

DEDICATIONS

This book is dedicated to Aoife, Ashleigh,
Debbie, Glen, Jo, Kate, Lena, Matt, Sammy and Sophia
for all your love, support and editing.

CONTENTS

ABOUT THE AUTHOR

Benjamin Daly is an acclaimed author and dating coach. For over a decade, he has helped women find and form relationships with their dream man. His study of behaviour, psychology and social interaction has led him to develop simple strategies that get results.

When he's not coaching, Benjamin devotes his time to his family, friends, fitness and food. You can find Benjamin on social media @benjamindaly.

DISCLAIMER

By reading this book, you agree to the following. You understand that the information contained in this book is an opinion and should be read for personal enjoyment only. None of the material in this book is to be considered medical, physical, psychological, sexual or legal advice, nor is this book intended to be a diagnosis, prescription, recommendation or cure for any kind of problem. For issues of a medical, physical, psychological, sexual and legal nature, always seek advice from a qualified professional.

You understand that you're wholly responsible for your own behavior and actions and agree to act ethically and abide by all laws. The author or publisher is not to be held responsible for the consequences of any irresponsible actions.

INTRODUCTION

What is this book about, and who is it for?

This book is a step-by-step guide to online dating for any woman who wants to find and form a relationship with their dream man. If you're reading this, you're probably frustrated and disappointed with the current dating scene, and wondering if there are even any decent guys out there. Fortunately, there are plenty, and I will help you find one just for you. No matter your current situation, previous experiences or feelings towards online dating, the pages of this book contain everything you will need to find, attract and date your future partner. My goal is to help get you into a long-term relationship with someone amazing, and I aim to get you there in less than 12 months.

It gives me great pleasure to provide advice from a male perspective. I will share with you some of the secrets behind how men think, what we are attracted to, how we interact and what makes us want to date someone and start a relationship. I will also highlight the most common mistakes women make that may be preventing them from getting the results they want. The information in this book is not common knowledge, so don't be too hard on yourself if you haven't had the best results so far.

What is this book *not* about?

This book is not about tricks and techniques. It's about core fundamentals. You will learn the principles that will help you succeed in finding a great guy and start a serious relationship. I've avoided all the fluff and got straight to the point as I know your time is precious.

I've also limited the scope of this book. Dating and relationships is a broad topic, which is why I've kept this book to online dating only. This book will take you through the stages before, during and after you're on the app.

What is online dating?

Today, online dating has become the primary means of connecting and communicating with potential partners. Whether you like it or not, it's here to stay. They may not be telling you, but according to research, 70% of single people have tried online dating.

You may have already had your own experiences with online dating, some good, some bad. If you haven't been getting the results you want, your approach will need to change. It's like playing a sport. If you keep losing, you're inevitably going to quit out of frustration. If you're winning, however, you will enjoy the experience and stick around long enough to achieve your goal. If you've been getting bad results, such as attracting the wrong type of guy, low engagement or interactions going cold, there's a reason why it's not working out. In this book, I'll expose the areas that are creating poor results for you, and how to fix them.

You can be reassured that these challenges are not exclusive to women. Men face exactly the same challenges too. Fortunately, online dating is a skill that can be learnt and mastered. It's like buying a piano and expecting to be a great pianist. You need to learn the skills and practice consistently until you get the results. Fortunately, when you learn how to date like a pro, you'll significantly improve your probability of success.

The most amazing thing about online dating is that it allows you to see and be seen by so many. In the not so distant past, single women would have interacted with only a handful of single men every week. Imagine how hard it would have been for your mom or your grandma. You've got it easy in comparison.

Nowadays, you have access to a gigantic database of age-appropriate single men in a matter of minutes. No other means of dating compares in its ability to pull so many singles together in such a fast and efficient manner. This allows you to connect with guys who you never would have connected with before.

Having this greater pool significantly improves your chances of finding Mr. Right. It's purely a numbers game—the more guys you can interact with, the greater the chance of finding a guy who ticks your boxes. It's the difference between fishing with a tiny little rod and a huge ocean trawl net. Studies even back this up: it has been found that marriages that begin online are less likely to end in break-up than relationships that were initiated through traditional means. Furthermore, they also offered a high rate of marital satisfaction. That is the beauty of choice. The more choice, the more likely you'll find a great match.

Why was this book written?

You might be wondering how this book came into existence. Over the years, I've noticed the amount of bad advice and limiting self-beliefs out there that hinder the success of many. Often this advice is dished out by single friends who are just as unsuccessful in their attempts to meet the right partner. You have to know where to get your advice. You probably wouldn't go to someone who's broke for money advice or someone who's unfit for nutrition and fitness advice, so why would you go to someone who's unlucky in love for dating and relationship advice?

The reason I have written this book is to provide useful and accurate information that's going to get you results quickly. The reason I know the answers is because being a man myself, I know what men like, don't like, and how men think. During my single years living in the city, I did an immense amount of online dating. I have seen it all, and then some. This experience has been invaluable, as I know first-hand what works and what does not.

Having this insider's knowledge will both help you attract a future partner and help contribute towards a happy, lasting and fulfilling relationship. The knowledge in this book will also help guide you away from the pitfalls that may have cost you time and caused you heartbreak in the past. Fortunately, you don't only have to learn through trial and error, like most do. By giving you the full end-to-end system, you will be able to expedite the process and avoid the unnecessary and painful mistakes along the way. Fortunately, finding and forming a relationship with the right guy is not all that hard if you know how.

What is the promise?

Success in dating and relationships is considered by most to be random, unpredictable and down to luck, but this is not true. Underpinning it all is a courtship process, and the courtship process has rules; unless you know how it all works, you're leaving it up to chance. Those who succeed are the ones who understand the rules and know how to navigate their way through successfully. Have you ever met someone who just seems to get 'lucky' every time? Whether they know it or not, they understand the system and know how to use it to their advantage.

In this book, I've written the process from start to finish that will enable you to understand how to get the result you need. By understanding the process, you will become an insider and benefit from all the opportunities that come your way. I want you to get to the point where there is an abundance of decent guys wanting to date you with the intention of forming a relationship. Like a commando, I want you in and out of dating as efficiently as possible, leaving only with your new man.

Before we get into the body of this book, I would like to highlight how significantly your mindset will affect your dating success. Almost every woman I meet who is having issues in this area carries negative beliefs about dating, relationships and men. Bringing a cynical attitude will only create a self-fulfilling prophesy. From my experience, the women who are most cynical or unwilling to change, suffer most. By carrying a negative attitude or being closed-minded, they become unteachable and the blockage to their own success. You'll significantly improve your chances of finding and forming a relationship with a great guy if you drop the negative beliefs weighing you down, make yourself open to change and have faith that it is possible.

Just as with anything else in life, the more you put in, the more you'll get out. To meet your man, it will require commitment, effort and persistence. It's like getting a great physique—you don't get fit by joining the gym, going twice then quitting because you didn't lose weight. You show up consistently. I will be like your personal trainer, building your programme. However, you will need to put in the work. Buying this book is not enough. Yes, you've taken the action to get help, but the value is in the process, not the event. You must apply what you've learnt.

The harder you work at it, the faster and better your results will come.

You must also be patient. Some people get lucky and find a guy very quickly, and I've seen this happen often. However, for most, it can take time. Dating is a numbers game and will require shuffling through the pack until you find your ace. Whatever you do, do not give up. You will definitely make mistakes and experience frustration, confusion, overwhelming odds and disappointment along the way; this is a normal part of the process. The key is to stick with it and have faith that your guy is around the corner looking for you too. If you quit you will <u>never</u> have the relationship you dream of. It's that simple.

Some of the worst advice that gets thrown around is that "you don't have to change a thing, just be yourself". It is true that we must be authentic to ourselves, but by not changing, we remain stuck. Ultimately, it's your beliefs and actions that have gotten you to where you are today. If you had the right beliefs and actions, you would be in a happy, fulfilling relationship with a great guy by now. You're going to have to change if you want a different outcome. As Einstein once said, "Insanity is doing the same thing over and over again, and expecting a different result." Everyone wants a better future, but most are not willing to change. You will need to change if you want this to work. I want you to wipe the slate clean, put your long-held beliefs in the bin and be open and willing to try out some fresh ideas and strategies.

You are the one who is in control and the only one who is responsible for your results. If you want the guy, you're going to have to put in the work. I want you to make a promise to do whatever it takes to make this happen. Nothing is guaranteed in life, but you can certainly have a significant influence on its direction. I want you to tilt the odds in your favor to give yourself the best chance of finding a great man. I can promise you, if you follow the guidelines in this book while keeping a positive, pro-active and patient attitude, you will find him. Your future self will thank you for the work you put in now.

Let's begin!

YOUR BRIEF

Your brief is the list of qualities that you want in the man you will be dating. You don't want just any guy, you want your dream guy. Therefore, you must be clear on the kind of person you want before beginning the search. There are a lot of guys out there, most of whom won't be suitable for you. If you are not specific from the start, you may match, date or even end up in a relationship with the wrong guy. This is a waste of your precious time and his, and often leads to confusion and upset when it ends— or worse, a long, unhappy relationship.

One of the biggest mistakes I see people make is taking a 'go with the flow' approach. This is when someone sets no standards and kind of just sees who shows up. By not being a chooser, you become the chosen, usually by someone who is not right for you. This typically ends in disaster. Like navigating a ship without a rudder, the chances of even making it out of port is unlikely.

From this point onwards, I want you to move in a straight line, not zig-zagging your way from one bad date or relationship to another. Be clear on your destination and head straight for it.

By setting clear standards, you will radically increase your chances of finding and maintaining a long-term relationship. This is because you reduce the chances of hitting road-blocks later down the line. Imagine that you meet a guy who you really like, but you discover that he doesn't want children and has no intention of having a family. If kids are what you've always wanted, then you have three options—you can either **accept it**, **change it** or **walk away**. Rather than accepting it or walking away, most women fall into the trap of trying to change it, which is a fruitless task. This is the reason why some relationships can be so draining. It's because you're trying to change someone who deep down doesn't want to change. Unfortunately, our emotional investment or fear of starting again keeps us in situations that aren't good for us. By far the simplest approach is to find someone else who is compatible, meets your needs, and will offer you an easier life with less friction. You want to swim with the current, not against it.

I've coached many women who have been in a bad relationship where they're faced with one problem after the next. There always seems to be some drama. They run themselves into the ground trying to change him or the situation to no avail. They eventually muster the courage to walk away in search of someone who's better capable of meeting their needs, and when this happens, instantly their life becomes easier. There is little drama and things move forward smoothly. A bad match is like wearing the wrong sized shoes—no matter how hard you try, they're never going to fit and it's going to hurt no matter what you do. When you finally switch them up for shoes that fit properly, you can once again move on without the discomfort. It's not to say that he's a bad person—he's just not the right fit for you, but he could be the perfect fit for someone else.

It takes a lot of courage to walk away from a bad situation, but if it was never going to work out in the long-term anyway, save yourself and him the time. You've got to remember, that by saying yes to Mr. Wrong, you're saying no to Mr. Right. Your Mr. Right is out there looking for you this whole time, but you've been busy with Mr. Wrong.

It's incredible what can happen when we are clear on what we're looking for. The universe has a way of giving us what we ask of it. I believe the law of attraction works because we plant a seed in our head, and this intention becomes a reference in our decision making. By saying yes to the right things and no to the wrong things, eventually we end up with what we want. By creating your brief, you're allowing the universe to work its magic.

However, don't expect your dream guy to rock up at your door with a bouquet of flowers. Finding and connecting with the right guy requires putting in the work. The key is to know what you want and take the actions necessary to make it happen. Dreams do come true, but you've got to give fate a helping hand.

I saw this happen first-hand when my older sister was finding herself in a string of bad relationships. Eventually I got her to write a list of all the qualities she wanted in a partner. After several months, she gathered the courage to leave her dead-end relationship, pick up her phone and get online. Soon after, she matched with her dream man. They are now married and starting a family. Recently she found her list at the bottom of her bag, and while reading it aloud discovered that the list was a description of her husband. This stuff really works—and yes, I'm taking full credit for helping her to find her soulmate!

By saying yes
to Mr. Wrong,
you're saying
no to Mr. Right.

Your brief is quite simply a list of the attributes you want in a guy.
These attributes could relate to these following areas:

- Personality *funny quirky*
- Values *Loving affectionate* *marriage= partnership*
- Physical appearance *tall*
- Education *big smile* *warm & unique eyes*
- Career *grad school?*
- Lifestyle *non smoker*
- Interests *College!* *movies*
- Social groups *savings* *art*
- Faith *minded* *science* *fantasy*
- Family preference *travel interest* *empathetic*
- Living situation *Career driven* *giving* *assertive*

We are all different, and you will have your own set of unique tastes
and requirements. Therefore, there are no right or wrong answers.
Your list is specific to you, and will depend on the type of guy you
want to date and eventually form a relationship with. Don't write
your list based on what other people want or what other people
want for you. Only you will know what would make a good fit.

There will also be attributes that you do not want. Knowing what
you don't want in a partner is a good step towards knowing what
you do want. Think back to your relationships that didn't work
out or the guys who weren't right for you. What traits did they
possess that you'd like to avoid? Keep this list positive and write
down the opposite qualities. For example, if you don't want a guy
who is lazy, write ambitious or career driven.

Your list might look as follows:

- *Kind* ✓
- *Funny* ✓
- *Taller than me* ✓
- *Wants kids*
- *Dark hair*
- *Intelligent* ✓
- *Athletic*
- *Generous* ✓
- *Wants marriage* ✓
- *Family orientated*
- *Ambitious* ✓
- *Nice eyes* ✓
- *Stubble*
- *Good job* ✓
- *Positive* ✓
- *Outgoing* ✓
- *Well dressed*
- *Loves running*
- *Courteous*
- *Confident*
- *Good arms* ✓
- *Good in bed* ✓
- *Well spoken* ✓
- *Assertive* ✓
- *Lives in my city*
- *Polite* ✓
- *Adventurous*
- *Likes to travel* ✓

Whatever your choice, it's imperative that you set your standards high. Don't let bad relationships lower your expectations. Aim for the best, someone amazing who adds value to your life and helps you to become a better person.

You might not be 100% certain on what you do want, and that's ok. This list will be a work in progress that you can adjust as you go. Be detailed in your preferences; this person will be a combination of everything you've ever wanted. Treat this as a shopping list. Imagine you could write this list, snap your fingers and there he appears. This is your "hell yes" kind of guy.

You might be tempted to skip or postpone this step. You've got to understand that writing your list is **the most** important part of the process, so do not skip this exercise under any circumstances. Write it now!

1) Kind / Empathetic / Polite
2) Funny ; Quirky ⚹
3) Taller than me 5'7⊕ ...
4) Intelligent (College Educated) ⚹
5) Generous
6) Marriage minded = Partnership ⚹
7) Ambitious
8) Nice eyes ; arms
9) Good job ; Career minded ⚹
10) Affectionate ; Attentive in/out of bed ⚹
11) Assertive
12) Interest in Travel, movies, novels fantasy
13) Good w/ money ⚹
14) Non smoker

15) Well spoken
16) Fit
17) Positive
18) Outgoing
19) Long hair
20)
21)
22)
23)
24)
25)
26)
27)
28)
29)
30)

"You'll never know what you can get until you've got it."

Now that you have your list, you are now going to use it as a reference point throughout the entire dating process. Make sure you have it on hand because you will be referencing back to it often.

As you know, nobody is perfect. Mr. Right will have his flaws, as will you in his eyes. Successful relationships work because both partners are happy to operate on a give-and-take basis when it comes to accepting one another's imperfections. The key is to know what's non-negotiable and what you're willing to allow.

I want you to go back to your list and star the characteristics that are the absolute must-haves. We all have our own sets of deal-breakers that deep down we know we could never compromise on. This process separates what you like from what you need. For example, wanting kids may be a must-have, while blue eyes and a passion for running is a bonus. By doing so, you are not compromising on your standards, you are instead allowing for a little flexibility.

Moving forward, you must take a firm stance on the must-haves, because if you date guys who don't have what you need, it will end in disaster and be a waste of time for both of you. You also can't claim that every attribute is a must-have. Sure, we don't want to settle for less, but we must be a little flexible; extreme pickiness will result in a futile search.

When you do start looking for someone, you'll find that most guys do not fit the bill, and that is ok. You are not looking for any guy, you are looking for *your* guy. Meeting the right partner is like finding a diamond in the rough, and to find Mr. Right, you will have to sift through a lot of Mr. Wrongs. This constant screening will happen all the way from the search, to the match, to the chat and to the date.

Knowing everything about a person based on their online profile is impossible; however, your brief will help you filter through what you do and do not want in the initial stages. By filtering based on your list, you will radically improve the chances of connecting with men who actually have the **potential** to be a compatible partner.

The key is having the discipline to say no. No matter how handsome he may be, if he doesn't match the must-have qualities you seek, move on. Remember looks and personality are not mutually exclusive, you can and will find the full package, it just takes work and a little patience.

You may find that you have to say one hundred no's for every one yes. The more you can say no, the better. Be abundant in your thinking, and have full faith that he's out there looking for you too.

Now that you have clarity in the guy you want to meet, I want you to close your eyes and imagine what it would be like to have this person in your life. What would it be like when the two of you go for dinner, go to parties, cook for one another, sleep in on a Sunday morning, spend Christmas with his family or take a holiday together?

Keep imagining these scenarios, regularly check in with these thoughts. Start making space for him in your life, leave some room in your wardrobe for his shirts and pick a side of the bed. I want you to manifest the shit out of this guy. He may not be here yet, but he's on his way.

There might be a little voice in the back of your head that says that this mystical man does not exist. The number of women I've worked with who are amazed that they were able to find their current partner is shocking. The fact is, you'll never know what you can get until you've got it. One day you will have met your partner and all the limiting beliefs about 'no good men' will disappear.

As a side-note: you must lose any baggage. If you're currently entertaining any guys who you know do not meet your list, you must let them go. Lose any 'special friends' or exes who are still lingering and not meeting your needs. Let them know that it's not going to work in the long term and you're ready to move on. Do this in a respectful manner. You might be emotionally invested in some of these guys, but I want you to be disciplined. Think of your future; if these interactions aren't going anywhere, what's the point? To allow the right guy to come into your life, you need to make space for him before his arrival.

SUMMARY

- Know what you want before you start
- A bad match is a bad match—you can either accept it, change it or walk away
- Write a list of all the attributes you want in a partner
- Your list is unique to you
- Be clear on what is essential and what is desirable

YOUR VALUE

To succeed in dating, you need to know how to sell your best qualities. How is a guy going to buy into you if you don't buy into yourself? You need to believe you're worthy of the best. If you believe you're worthy, he will too. If you don't, you'll subconsciously sabotage your success. A woman who has certainty in her own value knows that her presence is immeasurable in a man's life.

Think of the way studios sell a great movie to an audience. They don't tell you the movie has an average cast, mediocre storyline and sub-par production, then blow you away when you finally sit down to watch it. It's unlikely you'll ever watch the film because it was never something you would buy into in the first place. The movie industry knows that it needs to sell you on the movie well in advance. To effectively build hype, the trailer over-promises and then the movie over-delivers on that promise. I want you to take the same approach. You need to sell yourself as the best possible partner before you meet, and then do your best to over-deliver on your promises when you get together. By consistently over-delivering you not only continuously grow and improve the quality of your relationship, but you also continue to better yourself as a partner. This will inevitably grow your own self-worth and self-esteem.

Unfortunately, most women undersell themselves and do not acknowledge the tremendous amount of value they can offer as a partner. This may be because their qualities have gone unnoticed by themselves and others. Before we get into creating a profile, I want to get you to appreciate the value you can offer so that you never undersell yourself again.

For this exercise, I want you to write down a list of reasons why you'd make a great partner. This can range from the high-level attributes all the way down to the most detailed qualities. By completing this exercise, you'll gain a greater appreciation of all the amazing things you can offer in a relationship.

Here are some example qualities:

- *I am loyal* ✓
- *I have my own place* ✓
- *I have a great job*
- *I have awesome friends*
- *I am adventurous*
- *I know how to have fun* ✓
- *I'm a good listener* ✓
- *I have great hair* ✓
- *I'm pretty funny* ✓
- *I would make a loving mum*
- *I am honest*
- *I am excellent at interior design*
- *I'm an exceptional cook* ✓
- *I have a good relationship with my family*
- *I give the best advice*
- *I am very supportive* ✓
- *I look after myself physically*
- *I am super easy to live with*
- *I love to travel* ✓
- *I am smart with my money*
- *I take the time to look my best every day*
- *You can take me anywhere*
- *Etc.*

Writing 50 qualities can feel excessive, but I want you to keep going, only stopping when you hit that number.

Reasons why you'd make a great partner include:

1) I'm smart
2) I'm funny
3) I'm very approachable
4) I'm focused
5) I am loyal
6) I am creative
7) I'm a good listener
8) I'm a great conversationalist
9) I love to travel
10) I love learning new things
11) I am very supportive
12) I have my own place
13) I'm hard working
14) I'm goal oriented
15) I am affectionate
16) I am responsible

17) I have varied interests
18) I can be outgoing
19) I get along well with people
20) I am health conscious
21) I am kind
22) I am family oriented
23) I am dependable
24) I am passionate
25) I have beautiful hair
26) I have pretty eyes
27) I am charismatic
28) I am thoughtful
29) I am dedicated
30) I am loving
31) I am articulate
32) I am silly
33) I sing well
34) I'm a good planner
35) I give good advice

36) I am reassuring
37) I coordinate/decorate a space well
38) I am empathetic
39) I write well
40) I am positive
41) I make great friends
42) I am nurturing
43) I am educated
44) I am accomplished
45) I am resourceful
46) I am humble
47) I am inquisitive/curious
48) I am respectful
49) I am proud of my career
50) I am ambitious

I want you to start believing in yourself. Keep this list, read it often, and over time you will leave no doubt in your mind that you are a catch. Make it a goal to embed these positive self-beliefs into your psyche, until you have no hesitation regarding your own self-worth.

What I've found through my coaching is that the women who are most successful at attracting great guys, are those who can reel off their list without hesitation. These women are not arrogant, but they know their value, and everyone can sense it by the energy they're putting out. It's easy to spot those who know their own value. They typically walk and talk differently, and when they enter the room, people pay attention.

This belief changes the way you approach dating, giving you the confidence to go for the guys who you never thought would be interested. I want you to lead with the assumption that you are the best thing since sliced bread. After all, the world gives us what we believe we are. You don't have to be a show-off. You've just got to appreciate the value you have right now.

You are worthy of someone amazing, and remember, the right guy is out there searching for you too. If you don't appreciate your value right now, you won't sell him on the idea of being with you, doing both you and him a disservice.

It's important to appreciate your value right now, but we still have the capacity to grow and improve ourselves. We are all a work in progress. To increase your probability of success in dating and relationships, I want you to find areas in your life that you could improve upon. Think about your brief, where you specified your ideal man. What would he be looking for in a woman? Remember, to attract the best, you must become the best, and being the best makes you irreplaceable. This means we need to become what we want to attract.

I want you to write down a set of goals that will help you increase your value as a partner, along with the actions required to help get you there. Take inventory on where you're at, and find those areas that require some work. Your goals could be to get in shape, grow your network of friends, find a better job, increase your income, upgrade your wardrobe, move to a new house, start a hobby that you love, etc. Each of these goals should be followed up with measurable actions which can be implemented immediately.

For example:

GOAL	ACTIONS
Get in shape	Sign up to fitness class 3 times a week
	Remove all junk food and alcohol from the kitchen
	Do 10,000 steps minimum every day
	Drink 2 liters of water every day
	Eat 3 healthy meals every day

Please complete your own tables below:

GOAL	ACTIONS
Increase income	Cut excessive expenses
gain passive income
Start saving consistently
budget religiously
don't make unplanned purchases
establish style/look	buy clothes that interest me
buy outfits instead of indiv. items
take note of styles you like
make more time to get dressed
dress to be excited not to get it out of the way

19

GOAL	ACTIONS
Get in shape	Do 10,000 steps daily Yoga 2-3 x/wk Keep bread & junk food out house Eat more fruits & veggies Drink 64+ ounces of water

Once you have your immediate actions, you need to make them happen. Schedule them into your diary. Some may be one-offs and others may be repeating activities. Whatever they may be, ensure that you get them done. By working on your areas of improvement, it will give you greater confidence and increase your value as a partner. Once you've hit a goal, replace it with a new one.

SUMMARY

- You need to know how to sell yourself
- If you don't buy into yourself, neither will he
- Write down at least 50 reasons why you'd make a great partner
- Women who succeed in dating know their value
- Continue to grow your value as a partner
- Take action to progress your goals

YOUR APPROACH

Success in dating requires the right attitude. Unfortunately, many women carry negative beliefs about online dating and dating as a whole. This is understandable, as most women have had one or more bad experiences in the past. Trying to find a partner and a relationship while holding onto negative beliefs about men and dating is conflicting, like pushing the gas and the brake at the same time. You may already have some negative ideas about men and dating based on past experiences, but to move forward you will need to move beyond these preconceptions as they will only hold you back. From my own experience, the clients who struggle most are those who think they know it all, yet they remain single. Don't get in your own way!

Psychologists use the phrase 'projection is perception' to say that whatever you put out into the world is what you will see. If you believe the world is good, you will see goodness. On the other hand, if you project negative beliefs about men and dating, this is all you will see, further strengthening your negative beliefs. This is a vicious cycle. We need to break the negative beliefs and replace them with positive beliefs that help your cause. This is not blind optimism. It's about being objective, knowing that there is both good and bad, and then acting on the good opportunities when they arise.

Often, many of these limiting beliefs are excuses. They serve to avoid getting hurt, feeling uncomfortable, being rejected or putting in the work. You have a choice as to whether you buy into these excuses or not. You can have excuses or you can have results, but you can't have both.

You need to let go of all limiting beliefs, because they are unfounded, and the reason I know they are unfounded is because there are many women out there who have disproven these theories. These women are winning at dating and relationships because they don't allow these fallacies to come between themselves and their goal.

Harboring these negative beliefs has no value, because when you're in a relationship with a great guy, you are not going to think or care about those beliefs. They will all be a distant memory. So, don't waste your time on these nonsense excuses and instead direct your energy productively towards your goal.

Here are the most common limiting beliefs which may be hindering your success in finding a great guy:

"There are no good men out there"

The reality is, there are more than enough great guys who are single and open to starting a relationship with a great girl. You must operate from a mindset of abundance, not scarcity. In fact, never in history has it been easier to find a good guy. In the past, most relationships would form out of work, through friends, through school or in a bar. This meant your selection would have been extremely limited. We are so fortunate that the internet has revolutionized dating, and allowed us to open our phone and access a huge database of singles in our area within minutes.

Imagine how much harder it would have been for your grandma, and she still pulled it off, so please no complaining.

Yes, it's going to take some searching and sorting, but you'll find him if you're willing to put in the work. It's to be expected that not all guys are going to be suitable, so you will have to shuffle through the pack until you find the right one for you. If you live in a low population area where there really are few single men around, then you may want to move somewhere where there are more single men, like to the city. If getting a relationship is important to you, it might be the only option.

Dating is a numbers game. You may have had some bad experiences in the past, but this does not mean you'll have a bad experience in the future. Remember, you only need to find <u>one</u> great guy. And when you find him, this belief will become immediately obsolete.

"Men only want one thing"

It's true that sex is important to guys. However, most men would choose sex with one incredible partner who meets his needs over sex with multiple partners with whom he has no connection. Whether they realize it or not, most guys want what women want—a long-lasting, meaningful relationship with a partner who meets their needs. If you meet his needs as a partner, he will commit.

"All men cheat"

Some men do cheat, but some women cheat too. Cheating is a character flaw for those with low morals, regardless of gender. Being cheated on is horrible, but just because it's happened once doesn't mean it will happen again. Stereotyping in general is a bad idea as projecting an unfounded character flaw onto the right guy

YOUR APPROACH

will cause you to sabotage your opportunities. The guy you want to be with isn't a cheater because he has personal standards.

"I always attract the wrong type of guys"

There will be a lot of wrong guys out there. You can't expect them all to be right for you. However, you may find that you're attracting them. While there is nothing you can do about who is interested in you, there is something that you're doing that is allowing them in. By setting the brief for what it is you're looking for, you automatically exclude those that aren't right. You need to be able to spot red flags, and when you do, learn to disengage. The best apps allow for you to choose who contacts you so you can restrict the wrong guys from entering your space.

How you market yourself will also affect the type of guys you attract. If your photos are in any way suggestive, you'll invite the creeps and repel the upstanding gents. The reverse is also true, if you present yourself in a classy non-suggestive manner, the creeps won't bother and the right kind of guy will be drawn in. The energy you put out is what you'll attract.

Ultimately, you are the one in control of who comes into your space. If you're engaging with the wrong type of guys, it's a choice you've made. In the future, you will need to be more selective about who you let in.

"I'm focusing on me right now"

It's great to focus on other areas in your life. It could be your career, business, fitness, friends or travel. However, I must address the elephant in the room: Time does not stop. Life is like an escalator that's constantly moving, and if you want a family, you can't delay forever. We really need to make every day count.

I know this is uncomfortable to hear, but it's important that we address it now. If you want a family, you will need a partner, and to find a partner you need to be dating. Dating is what scientist call a 'delayed return environment'. This means that the results of your decisions will only be felt later. If you choose to opt out of the dating, you will not notice any negative effects today. However, this inaction today may cause you problems several years from now. If you're not prioritizing dating, you will only increase the pressure later down the line. The key is to dig the well before you're thirsty, so don't leave it too late!

Fortunately, you can find a way to make it all work at the same time. The key is to prioritize what is both urgent and important and deprioritize what is not. Taking immediate action will make you feel better as you know you are doing something productive towards the outcome you want.

"I'm taking a break from dating"

If you've recently come out of a relationship, it's a good idea to take some time to reflect on the situation before you go back out there again. However, as we discussed previously, time is of the essence. If you fast forward to when you're in a happy relationship, you're not going to care about previous relationships. Therefore, don't let a break up slow you down from finding the right guy.

If you're taking a break simply because you're not getting results, you need to change your approach. Believe me, when you get good results, the last thing you'll want to do is stop.

"You can have excuses, or you can have results, but you can't have both."

"I don't want to get hurt"

It's natural for us to avoid getting hurt, especially if you've been hurt in the past. We all feel fear, and men fear rejection as much as you do. There is always an inevitable level of risk involved in starting something new, and there is always a chance that you'll get rejected or heartbroken. But there's also a chance you'll meet the love of your life and be in a happy relationship. Remember, the pain of rejection is nothing compared to the pain of regret, so never cower. Discomfort is the entry price to success. You must be willing to push through the heartbreak to get to your destination.

Even if you do everything right, there are still no guarantees, as you can still get hurt and disappointed. Just know that if you do get rejected or heartbroken, you'll be ok. We are built to handle rejection. If we weren't, our species would have died out a long time ago. Knowing that everything will be ok will give you the confidence to take the risk. If he does reject you, know that there is a great guy around the corner who will love and cherish you. You may experience 10 heartbreaks, but the 11th guy could be the one who loves you forever.

"It's not going to last"

There are a multitude of reasons why a relationship or date would fail. I could tell you to be positive and that positivity will cure all, but this isn't going to solve your problem. If things never seem to last, and failed relationships happen often, this is a sign that there may be issues that need to be resolved. It could be with him—namely that you're picking the wrong type of guys—or it could be you, in which case you need to learn what is putting guys off and what you need to do to fix it. It may be a blend of the two. Underlying every success is a formula, whether that be for getting fit, getting rich or getting into a relationship. By understanding the formula for successful dating, you will significantly improve your probability of finding and keeping a good one.

"I'm ok on my own"

It's great to be self-sufficient, but it's also great to share your life with an incredible partner. The healthiest relationships are those where neither partner is dependent on one another. They are emotionally and financially self-sufficient. They are together because they want to be together, not because they need to be together. Being with the right partner is synergistic, whereby 1+1=3. You can create and become far more than you are individually. Although you may not technically need a man, there's no reason not to look for someone incredible and build an epic life together.

"Guys online are weirdos"

Yes, there are weirdos online, but the internet is just a microcosm of society. There are weirdos in the real world, but certainly no more and no less online. Everyone uses dating apps, the good and the bad. It's not like all the decent guys don't use their mobiles to date, because believe me, they do.

Fortunately, you have the power to disengage from all the guys who aren't right for you and instead focus your energy on the good ones. Your job is not to change anyone, but to simply avoid the wrong ones until you find your diamond in the rough.

"I just want to meet guys the natural way"

Finding a guy the 'natural' way, is like finding a job the 'natural' way. It might happen, but it will probably take you 10x longer. Like with a job, you have to get out there and make it happen, you can't expect it to come to you. Believe me, the woman who is proactive is the one snapping up the great guy right now.

If you're against online dating, you're going to make finding a man so much harder for yourself. Online dating is the easiest and most efficient way to date. Having the ability to get in front of thousands of local singles 24 hours a day is nothing short of a miracle. However, many people turn their nose up and opt for the 'natural' approach. The probability that your dream man will show up at your work, the supermarket or the launderette is slim. To hell with fate, you've got to maximize all your opportunities and make it happen for yourself. The more you put in, the more you'll get out. It's that simple.

Finding your dream man is a numbers game, and the more guys you can get in front of, the more likely it is that you'll meet him. You want to be working with a big pool of singles. Offline, you might meet a small handful of single men each week, while online you can be seen by thousands. Selecting from a small pool of men will take you an eternity and you don't have the time to waste. Make probability work to your advantage and do both. Those that succeed in anything are those who maximize all opportunities that come their way. Therefore, if you do happen to run into a guy in the coffee shop, go and make conversation.

Now I want you to fast forward to relaxing on the sofa on a Sunday with your dream guy. Do you think you'll care whether you met him online or in a coffee shop? How you met does not matter. It doesn't take long for an online interaction to manifest into the real world. Therefore, don't let your drive for meeting him romantically prevent you from meeting him in the first place. The priority is to form a relationship with your dream man, not the story you tell your grandkids. Yes, it's true, online dating is not the most romantic scenario. However, online dating is purely a means of arranging a face-to-face interaction. Once you've met that special someone, that's when the fairy tale can begin.

As a side note, please no complaining that technology has ruined romance. If you do form a long-term relationship, the period you share online may make up 0.001% of your time together, leaving you ample time in the real world to get romantic.

"If I look for it, I won't find it"

This belief that looking for something will cause it to evade you is totally nonsensical. If you want something, you must go get it. Finding the right partner is a numbers game. If you put yourself in front of 1,000 single men, you're that much more likely to find the right guy. Leaving it all to fate is the passive approach which will take you a long time, and it may be too late by the time you find him. You can't take the risk. Remember, he is looking for you also, and if you can't be found, you will never cross paths.

"Online dating is desperate and embarrassing"

Online dating is now considered the norm. Due to its rapid adoption into the mainstream, it's no longer stigmatized. Most singles are now online. If you feel online dating is desperate or embarrassing, you are hindering your own success. To get the best results, you must let go of the feeling that it is somehow beneath you.

If you are concerned about how your friends will think of it, you need to put it into context. What do you value more, the opinion of others or the opportunity to find your dream man? Have the confidence to put yourself out there without shame. Those who judge will likely be single themselves. Tell them that you're going to find your guy and that you'll do whatever it takes to find him. The best results come to those who take advantage of opportunities. Ultimately, you can be self-righteous or you can be in a relationship.

"I don't have time for dating"

We all lead busy lives, but you must make time if you want the results. It's a matter of prioritizing. All you need is one hour a day. This is enough time to search, chat with and date guys who have potential. See this as an investment in the future. It will take time, but in the end it will be worth the sacrifice when you're in a relationship with a great guy. Your love life is too important to postpone or abandon.

One huge advantage is that online dating allows you to search from the comfort of your own home. In the past, you had to actually get dressed to meet men. Now you can match, talk and arrange dates with guys while in your PJ's. Genius!

If you're spending your time on mindless activities that aren't moving you forward in your love life, such as watching back-to-back TV series, being hungover or spending idle time on social media, you will have to re-prioritize until you get the results you want. You might find that you're working crazy hours at work and don't have time. If this is the case, you might need to change your job to something that allows you the time to date and form a relationship. Sometimes we must make sacrifices, and you've got to decide which is more important.

Another huge drain on time is overthinking. If you're spending copious time thinking or talking to friends about a guy who won't commit or a guy who let you down, then you must find the discipline to move on.

Throughout the process, I want you to always be asking the question: "Is this activity helping me find and form a relationship with my dream man?" If it's not, stop doing it and replace it with something that's going to push you toward your goal.

"I'm not ready to date"

There are a ton of reasons why you may not feel ready to date. It may be that you just came out of a relationship, or you want to focus on other areas and only want to start dating when things are just right. The reality is that there is no 'right time'. Waiting until you're over him, moved out, in your new job or lost 5lbs is only a delaying tactic. There's never a perfect time to be meeting people.

A friend of mine came out of a relationship and got online almost immediately. She had her doubts but she knew she had to move on. Within seven days of the breakup, she met her dream man and they are now happily married. These things do happen, but they only happen when you stop procrastinating and take action. Stop waiting for the perfect time and start now.

"I'm scared"

It's normal to feel scared. Putting yourself out there is not the most comfortable feeling in the beginning. Remember, your brain is designed to protect you from harm, therefore anything out of the familiar creates a biological reaction that makes you want to retreat. Unfortunately, if we are to grow, we need to expand our comfort zone and get comfortable being uncomfortable. This means acknowledging the fear and doing it anyway.

The best way to overcome a fear is to immerse yourself in it until it becomes familiar. Psychologists call this immersion therapy. If you fear dating, go on more dates. It's that simple.

I'd also advise spending more time with guys in general. Even if you have no interest in dating these men, by making more male friends, you will become more comfortable interacting with guys and the fear will soon subside.

"No one excites me"

You may not have found the right guy yet, but he's out there. Dating is a numbers game; you must go through a lot of 'No's' until you find a Yes. Remember, you only need one guy, not a hundred. Using your brief, you can target who you want, then spend time searching and engaging with potentials. You will find him—you just have to trust the process.

"Online dating is superficial"

A lot of people say that online dating is all based on looks. It is true that your first impression is based on physical appearance, but this has always been the case, long before online dating even existed.

The point is, you want it all. You want a man you're physically and emotionally attracted to, who is also physically and emotionally attracted to you. You do not have to choose between looks and personality, you can have it all. Being physically attracted to your partner is necessary, so embrace it.

"Online dating makes people so disposable."

Whether this is true or not, I don't know. Society may have changed as a result of this technological change, or it might not have. Either way, it doesn't matter. Your job is to find a decent guy and exit the dating scene completely. Instead, concern yourself on the areas that you can control, like the amount of effort you put towards finding your man.

"It's just so much effort"

Finding your dream guy will take some work. Some will get lucky early, but most will have to put in work to make it happen. You may have downloaded the app, put up a couple of photos, and you maybe even got as far as sending a couple of messages. If this is you, then you're half-assing it. It's like dipping your toe in the water rather than jumping in. Ask yourself the question: how much you really want it?

You must make the commitment and keep working until you get results. Even if it takes 1,000 dates, keep showing up. Quitting is not an option, unfortunately. Yes, it will take effort to talk and date, and you may have to do a lot of dating, but it's worth the investment. Nothing great is going to fall into your lap unless you make the commitment to do whatever it takes to find your guy. Remember, mediocre action creates mediocre results. If you want the relationship, you've got to go get it!

CHALLENGE:

In the table below, write down the negative beliefs and excuses which are preventing you from succeeding in dating, and then come up with a list of reasons why they are unfounded:

NEGATIVE BELIEF OR EXCUSE	REASONS WHY IT IS UNFOUNDED
I attract weirdos	Just because that's been true in the past doesn't mean it's true for my future.

NEGATIVE BELIEF OR EXCUSE	REASONS WHY IT IS UNFOUNDED
I'm fat & unattractive right now	I'm not happy w/ my body but that doesn't mean a guy would be uninterested or a real block
Guys just want to use me for sex	Some do because I've historically allowed them too
The guys I like are too hot for me	I don't know that because I don't talk to them
I don't feel inherent attraction to guys	That's because I haven't made a real connection with the right guy

> Mediocre action creates mediocre results.

THE APP

There are multiple online dating apps to choose from, and they all vary in features and format. Some involve swiping while some do not, some have questionnaires and some limit communication.

Despite these differences, the same fundamental principles apply to all of them. Therefore don't get too hung up on the platform itself. If you have a great profile, you will generate the right kind of interest, no matter which platform you choose.

To maximize your exposure and opportunities, select an app that the most people use. New platforms are always popping up, so research the most popular at the time you're looking. Typically, the mainstream apps are the most user friendly and yield the best results.

Apps with a good reputation and a strong focus on relationships are ideal. On the other hand, be mindful that apps vary wildly in reputation. A dick pic is often a form of hello on some online platforms, so choose wisely. To safeguard against the penis invasion, some apps only allow women to message first. This means you will only be in communication with the guys you want to communicate with.

I'd recommend sticking to one or two excellent platforms where a lot of men are active. Using more than two platforms will spread your attention. Taking the trial and error approach to platforms will help you find one which you like best.

Most apps are now free with paid extras. By paying, you can unlock additional features which may offer benefits. It's often worth paying extra to have the additional features, however, this does not guarantee you success. A great profile and good chat is what gets dates, so you can still find Prince Charming while remaining thrifty.

SUMMARY

- Choose a popular, reputable app where most singles congregate
- The app is not as important as having an amazing profile
- Stick to one or two apps

CHALLENGE:

If you haven't already downloaded an app, I want you to download one now. Google 'best dating app' if you're unsure about which one's the most popular.

YOUR PROFILE

Now, this is the big one. Your profile is the page which is presented to others on the platform. Think of it as a brief snapshot of you and your life. Different apps have different features, but most at least include the following:

- Photos
- Bio
- Other features depending on app

Your profile is what gives you the opportunity to sell the guy of your dreams on the idea that you are the only one he should be pursuing as a partner.

To give you an example, there are moments as a guy when you stumble upon a girl's profile, and become so blown away that you want to cancel all plans and focus fully on this one perfect angel. Your mind starts ticking and you start planning your future with this person you have never met or even matched with. You thought only women do this, right? In the following chapter, we are going to build a profile for you that has this same effect.

To achieve this, you must first know how to market yourself. I want you to think of yourself as a brand. I want you to take care of your brand the way designer labels like Chanel or Hermes take care of theirs. I want you to imagine your profile as a shop window. If your shop window is a mess, no matter how many people walk past, very few will show interest. If, however, your shop window is eye catching and beautifully presented, it is likely that the people walking past will take notice and walk in. Ultimately, your ability to match with the right kind of guy rests on the quality of your profile.

We are all in sales, every second of the day, and not all sales are financial. Think about it—you had to sell yourself to your boss, you had to sell yourself to your landlord, you even had to sell yourself to your best friend. Once they're sold on you, you must sell them every day to maintain that status. If you perform badly at work, stop paying your rent or abandon your friends, the sale is over. This also works in return: your boss, landlord and best friend had to sell themselves to you too. Dating and relationships are no different. I realize that this sounds unromantic, but it is the truth. Ultimately, relationships are an exchange of needs—he can provide you with something you want and you can provide him with something he wants. The reason why relationships don't work is because one or both parties aren't able to fulfill a need. By understanding the concept, you will rapidly improve your likelihood of finding and keeping the right guy.

To get the guy, you must sell yourself as a valuable partner for him to invest in you. However, this is not a one-way street. He must equally sell himself to you also. Your profile is where it begins, and you must use your profile to sell him on the idea of making you his girlfriend.

There are many other women online, therefore you must stand out from the crowd if you want to generate interest. If you're not standing out, you're invisible. You only have a few seconds to pique his interest so you must make an impact in that short time. The brain is designed to make assumptions about others quickly. We must make sure your profile paints you in the most positive light.

Since you've never experienced what it's like being a guy on dating apps, you are unlikely to have any insights into what most women's profiles are like. First, most girls know what visually makes a good photo, and these photos are beautifully taken. However, the photo content is usually bland and uninspiring. The selection is also highly predictable. Most profiles contain the same type of photo, and jumping between one profile to another can be like a game of spot the difference. Bios are the main area of weakness for most women. They are usually bland, predictable or non-existent.

This presents a huge opportunity for you to build a profile that stands out in the sea of mediocrity. You can achieve this by building a profile that is different from the rest.

Like you, the right kind of guy will be selective. He doesn't really want to waste his time with the wrong type of girl. The reality is, while looking at your profile, he too will be looking for reasons to say no. Never give him a reason to say no. Always be his 'hell yes'. You want to make him excited about the prospect of matching, dating and forming a relationship with you.

The beauty of setting yourself apart from the crowd is that you can be uniquely you. We all have something wonderful to offer, your job is to communicate your uniqueness through your profile. You can share the aspects of your personality, interests, passions and goals that make you different from everyone else.

"If you're not
standing out,
you're invisible."

The benefit of this is that you don't have to pretend to be someone you're not. You can in fact use your profile to celebrate what makes you different rather than trying to blend in like everybody else. You're a wolf, not a sheep.

Most people don't spend enough time crafting their profile, and it's obvious in the finished product. This is such a waste of an opportunity. I want you to build and refine your profile with care to maximize your opportunities.

For a successful profile, all components must be high-quality and working to sell you as the partner he's been looking for. You do this by creating a profile that is fun, interesting and unique. Boring and predictable is what kills attraction. Your profile must also match with who you are so that when you walk through the door on your first date, your virtual self matches your actual self.

Why is it paramount that your profile is congruent with your reality? Living a life of passion, purpose, connection, adventure and fulfillment is the objective. Your profile should be a snapshot of the awesome life you live. It's like a resume that highlights your personality, interests and values. Ultimately, if you want to attract a guy who has it all going on, he will expect the same of you.

In the following chapters, I'll show you how to create a remarkable profile that projects an accurate and powerful image of yourself, setting you apart from all the rest.

SUMMARY

- You profile will make or break your success online
- You must sell yourself through the cultivation of a compelling profile
- Most women's profiles are boring and predictable
- It's easy to stand out from the crowd
- Never give him a reason to say no
- You want to communicate your uniqueness
- Your profile must be accurate and congruent

YOUR PHOTOS

Photos are by far the most important part of your profile. Data published by OkCupid estimates that photos drive 90% of the action.

Men are highly visual. Almost every study conducted on attraction has revealed the same conclusion: a woman's appearance is what triggers a man's attraction receptors. We are biologically programmed to be attracted to women who will give birth and raise healthy offspring. Qualities that trigger attraction include clear skin, bright eyes, full lips, healthy hair, large breasts and a good hip-to-waist ratio. As superficial as they may seem, these traits are biological signs of fertility. Through evolution, the male brain is designed to scan women quickly for visual signs of fertility. As the saying goes, "A man falls in love through his eyes."

This doesn't mean that you must look like a Victoria's Secret model to find success online. There's a big difference between objective beauty and perceived beauty. The key is to present yourself in the best possible way to set off the guy's attraction triggers.

Through photos, not only will he be able to see how you appear physically, he will also have an insight into your lifestyle and personality. The goal is to convey all sides of your persona. This allows him to get to know a little about you before you speak.

Like attracts like, therefore people are attracted to those that are like themselves. If you want to attract the guy outlined in your brief, you need to curate your photos to match him. For example, if you're adventurous and you want an adventurous guy, don't put up six photos of yourself hanging out in bars. Remember, you will attract what you put out.

Once you have your amazing selection of photos locked down, you will generate a lot of attention. As mentioned earlier, the more guys you can attract, the greater your options and the more likely you are to find someone suitable.

Everyone is different, so use this opportunity to stand out from the crowd. Even while following the set of guidelines I provide, I want you to demonstrate your uniqueness within these parameters.

It is paramount that you curate your profile carefully. Every photo needs to communicate your best qualities. Most platforms will limit the number of photos you can upload, usually to a maximum of six to eight. Therefore, I'd recommend that you use all the spaces available. If you have filled all the photo spaces with great photographs, it communicates that you have an abundance of great photographs and he will want to see more.

There is a selection of photos which you must include. These are:

The close-up photo

This one is going to be your main photo, the initial impression that people see, because first and foremost a guy wants to actually see what you look like. It's imperative that you get this one right as this one single photo will have the biggest impact on the interest you generate. To make this photo work, it will need to clearly show your face and shoulders, and if possible, your upper body. It's important that you look natural. Smiling is a good option as it will make you appear more approachable. A selfie is allowable for your close-up if you look happy and affable. The photo should include yourself **only** and the background of the photo should be clean and not distracting. Ensure that you are well dressed and looking great.

The full body photo

This is a photo of your whole body. This allows him to see you from head to toe. Smiling is an option, but not necessary.

The photo should be of yourself **only** and the background of the photo should be clean and aesthetic. You might have this photo taken before a social event when you are looking your best. It's ok to wear something that shows off your figure but make sure it's not too revealing; subtlety is key. You want to leave it to his imagination. If you're posting more than one of these photos, remember to have a balance between dressed up and casual. If you're dressed up in every photo, he might think that you are high maintenance. Wearing something casual shows your easy-going side.

The social photo

This is a photo of you in your social environment. It may be a photo of you with friends or family. This demonstrates your sociability and family connections. He wants to see that you have a social life and a good group of people around you. This photo could be taken at a party, a wedding or on holiday. You do not want too many people in the photo as this can be overwhelming and distracting. Between two and four people, including yourself, is the maximum. Do not have more than one social photo in your profile—remember, he wants to see **you**, not all your friends and family. Ensure that the environment of this photo is clean and inviting, and ensure everybody in the photo is well presented and represents you well.

The active photo

This is a photo of you doing something active that you enjoy. For example, it could be you doing your yoga, horse riding, dancing or hiking, if that's your thing. A photo of you partaking in your hobbies and interests is an amazing way to show a different side of your personality. It's attractive for a guy to see that you have a life you value and enjoy. The more exciting your life is, the more he will want to share it with you. Make sure that you are a significant feature in the photo, never be a dot on a mountain. A bikini photo will always generate interest, but keep it classy. If you want to include a bikini photo, make sure it's taken somewhere appropriate like a beach, pool or boat.

The random photo

This is a photo of you doing something funny or interesting. This could be a selfie of you with a 90s celebrity, dressed up as a Disney character or holding an otter while at the zoo. The options are endless. The random photo shows that you don't take yourself too seriously and serves as a great conversation starter. When a guy matches with you, he's scratching his head thinking of something to say. By having a photo with a story, it makes it easy for him to ask questions and for you to respond.

In terms of order, the close-up photo should always be your main image and the random photo at the end should help lead into conversation. The quality of these photos is important. All photos must be well lit (natural light preferably), evenly cropped, clear and high quality, taken on a decent camera or camera phone.

There are certain photos that you must avoid as they are detrimental to your goal of generating interest. Even if you have five great photos, the one bad photo can easily put a guy off. These bad photos include:

The mirror selfie – Mirror selfies are often taken in the bedroom, bathroom or gym mirror. It involves little creativity and he may assume that you are self-involved. Not a great look.

The other guy – Photos with another guy cause unnecessary confusion as it can be misinterpreted as an ex. This even applies to photos with a male friend, colleague or brother, because at first glance, no one knows what this person means to you. It's best to avoid this situation completely. It also goes without saying that photos of you with your ex should never appear on your profile or social media while dating online.

The infant – A photo of you with someone else's kids or baby can be cute, but this too can send out mixed messages. Some guys might assume that the child is yours, which brings up unnecessary questions. If you do have kids, it's up to you whether you want to include your children in your photos.

The crowd – It's good to include a social photo, but avoid photos of vast crowds. This type of photo is confusing as it's hard work figuring out which one is you. He wants to see you, not your netball team. Remember, four people max people per photo, including yourself.

The exposed – It's ok to show off your figure but don't go overboard. Too much cleavage or photos from behind will generate attention, but this will be from the wrong type of guys. The right guy will be turned off by revealing photos. He's looking for someone to settle down with, not an attention seeker. There's nothing more attractive than a girl who's in great shape but leaves it to his imagination. Subtlety is the key.

The blurred – This is a phenomenon whereby the face of a friend in a photo is pixelated or blurred. It's understandable that you may not want to include your friend's face, but this makes your friend look like they're in witness protection. It's best to find another photo or find a friend who doesn't mind having their photo featured.

The inconsistent crop – Having a selection of photos in a variety of different sizes and crops look messy. Try to keep your photos to the same crop for tidiness as it shows you take care of how your profile is presented.

The deja vu – This is when a selection of similar photos are used consecutively, usually at the same location but at slightly different angles. An example would be three virtually identical selfies, or four consecutive bedroom mirror selfies. This demonstrates an intense lack of creativity and doesn't display the other areas of your life.

The grainy – Images which are low quality or grainy should not be featured on your profile. This usually occurs when images are heavily cropped or taken on a bad camera. These photos look bad. Only clear, high quality photos should feature on your profile.

The darkness – These are photos which are poorly lit. These photos should be avoided as they look uninviting. Ensure that all photos on your profile are well lit. It's best that most of your photos are taken during the daytime.

The mess – Any photo which includes a dirty or messy background such as an unmade bed or dishes in the sink. This looks unappealing. Make sure the backgrounds of your photos are clean and tidy.

The throwback – No photos older than 18 months should be featured. Old photos can be misleading if you look different now compared to when the photo was taken.

The other stuff – This is a photo of anything but yourself. This can include a quote, your dog, a meme or a random sunset. Every photo on your profile must include you and your face.

The intoxicated – It's ok to be holding a drink in a photo, but make sure this is the exception. If every photo features a drink, he's going to think you're a party girl.

The ignited – Smoking is also very offputting for most guys. Smoking isn't good for your health and should certainly not be featured on your profile.

The filtered — Filters that make you look like a dog, angel or flower girl aren't going to make the cut. A guy wants to see you looking natural and like an adult.

The pout – Pouting is not a good look, but for some reason it has become the norm. A natural expression or a relaxed smile wins hands down every time.

The opulent – Having photos which are all taken in the best restaurants, at the most luxury holiday resorts or in the most expensive designer clothes sends out a message that you are someone who appreciates the finer things in life. That's fine if you are looking for a man who appreciates the same things, but most guys would likely perceive you as shallow and high maintenance.

The faceless – This is when your face is covered, which includes the hats and sunglasses. You may not like having photos taken, but unfortunately, you need to show your face to get dates.

The obscure – This is when the profile includes only one or two photos. This communicates that you have something to hide. He may also assume that your profile is a catfish. If you are not willing to make the effort, neither will he.

The extra obscure – This involves literally no photos and goes without saying that it would throw up red flags to any guy.

The alternative – This includes photos which are overly artistic and alternative. This comes across as try hard, pretentious and aloof. He wants to see clear photos of you without all the mystery.

The man hater – Any photos which berate men are a huge turn off. This include t-shirts or neon signs with slogans that undermine the male gender. You don't want to put out those vibes as it goes against what you're trying to achieve.

The professional – This involves any overly professional photos, usually taken in a photo studio with extra photoshopping. Professional studio photos are good for your LinkedIn, but not for your dating profile. It's best to keep it natural.

If you don't have photos which meet the guidelines above, be proactive in facilitating situations where photos can be taken. Use holidays, weddings, parties or any other event as an opportunity. If you have nothing booked in the diary, make plans. Good photos are a numbers game, the more photos you take, the more likely you'll find one you like.

The key is to be highly ruthless in your photo selection. Every photo needs to add value to your profile; if it doesn't add value, don't include it. Remember, photos drive 90% of the action, so it's worth making the investment in getting it right.

It's a good idea to run your profile by several trusted male and female friends. A fresh set of eyes can show you how someone else might see your profile differently.

Once your profile is live, it's worth rotating your photos to keep your profile fresh. You might find that one photo is a showstopper that drives a lot of interest. In that case, don't change a thing.

It can take time to build a portfolio of great photos. However, a lack of great photos should not prevent you from starting. Do your best for now and change them up later. See it as a work in progress—commit first, figure the rest out later.

If you need an opinion, upload your photo to Instagram and tag me @benjamindaly. I'll review and comment with my thoughts.

SUMMARY

- Photos make up 90% of the action and are the most important element of your profile
- Curate photos that match you and your lifestyle
- Add new photos and rotate to see which create the most engagement

CHALLENGE:

Upload your best photos to your profile now with a view to improving your photos over time.

THE BIO

Your bio is the part of you profile where you can describe yourself in few words that summarize who you are. Traditionally this has been a blank text box in which you can write whatever you'd like. However, many apps now encourage users to answer specific questions, which then feature on their profile. Whatever the format, the same principals apply.

A bio serves two purposes:

- To communicate information about yourself that will get him interested in you.
- To facilitate a fun and engaging conversation.

By describing yourself in an entertaining and compelling way, you're giving him an insight into your lifestyle and personality. This is your opportunity to sell yourself as the fun and interesting person that you are. The more exciting your life is, the more attractive you will become. You want the guy to be thinking, "Not only does that girl look incredible, but she seems fun too."

An interesting bio will create what are known as hooks; these are points in your bio which can be easily turned into conversation. Hooks initiate intrigue and lead to comments and questions.

When a guy comes across a bland, generic or short bio, it's very difficult for him to find anything to comment on or ask questions about. Even if he's a good conversationalist, he will struggle if he has nothing it work with. Most of the time he's scratching his head thinking, "What do I say?" This is incredibly frustrating. If it's too hard to open a conversation, he will likely move on to the next profile or start with something generic like, "Hey, how's your weekend?", which instantly sets the conversation down a boring and predictable road. You need to ensure that your bio is loaded with hooks for easy, fun and interesting conversation to flow.

Most women's bios are short, generic, uninspiring or non-existent, which is such a shame. However, this is a huge advantage for you as it's very easy for you to stand out from the crowd.

In this chapter, I will share with you the formula for writing the perfect bio that will grab his attention and make him want to know more. Before we do that, here's a list of the most common bio mistakes women make that must be avoided:

The bewildered – This is a bio which usually starts with 'I don't really know what I'm doing on this' or 'My friend signed me up to this thing'. This shows low commitment and doesn't come across as authentic.

The speechless – This one usually includes 'I don't know what to write' or 'I'm not sure what to say'. This one gets a 0 for effort. He will assume that conversation will be difficult if you can't think of anything to say about yourself.

The overtly sexual – This usually contains something which is suggestive such as 'I give great massages'. The right guy will think this is desperate.

The expeditor – This is a bio which encourages speed. It will usually contain phrases like 'I need a good man quick!' or 'My biological clock is running out'. This also comes across as desperate.

The deal breaker – This one usually involves multiple clauses, such as 'No players', 'No games' and 'Time wasters need not apply'. Of course, nobody wants these things, but declaring it brings a negative, high maintenance vibe and the right guy will be turned off.

The uninspired – This one involves minimal effort. Usually containing a short question such as 'How are you?' or 'What do you want to know?'. The right guy will not entertain this as the conversation will likely be equally as uninspiring.

The animated – The odd emoji to liven up your bio is acceptable, but 14 emojis back-to-back as a description is not, as this will make you look immature. Keep emojis to a minimum.

The obvious – This involves generic interests like 'Cocktails with the girls', 'Shopping' and 'Staying at home watching movies'. These statements feature on most women's profiles. What woman doesn't like those things? You need to be different. Remember, boring and predictable is the death of attraction.

The desolate – Having an empty bio signifies low investment and comes across as lazy and aloof. A guy typically won't bother communicating if it's too hard for him to start a conversation and build rapport, he will just go elsewhere.

The package deal – If you have kids that's fine, and it's a great idea to disclose it in your bio for transparency, but making paternal demands on the man whom you've never met will scare him off.

The list – This involves a long list of generic verbs and nouns such as 'shopping, family, travel, my dog, gin, eating out, wine, movie nights'. Lists are uninspiring, generic and require little imagination.

The preacher – This one usually takes the form of ranting about certain held beliefs, such as veganism. Although the cause can be for good, the approach comes across as judgmental and inflexible.

The downer – This is a bio that contains negative self-talk. A little self-deprecation can be amusing, but only when said in a non-serious manner. If you describe yourself negatively and you mean it, this will turn a man off. You must be positive about yourself. If you can't love yourself, it will be hard for him to love you.

The philosopher – Including any kind of quote is a no. This is unoriginal and doesn't add any value to your profile.

The best bios are those which are descriptive in an interesting and playful manner. It is also loaded with hooks which make it easy for the guy to initiate conversation.

To make your bio stand out, you must think creatively. Here are examples of two sentences conveying the same information in two very different ways:

1) I'd love to learn to cook one day.

2) My cooking is a health hazard, please teach me.

1) I love walking my dog.

2) I am a dog-mom to my 6-month old puppy Roxie.
Walkies are our thing.

1) I like chilling and watching movies at the weekend.

2) My typical Sunday involves watching trilogies.
Back to the Future, Toy Story, Spider-Man.
I've got it covered.

1) I am a shoeaholic.

2) I have a weakness for Christian Louboutin.
Just too many shoes, not enough feet.

As you can see, description 1 is boring and predictable. Description 2 however, is fun, interesting and encourages further questions. It's simply a case of re-wording your description from the mundane to the sublime. It's more important how you say it than what you say. The second descriptions also give more detail; by providing more specific information you give him more to ask questions about while demonstrating openness. Openness creates familiarity and familiarity gets the conversation going.

The ideal bio is one paragraph. It should be long enough to pull him in, but short enough to leave him wanting to know more. You don't have to explain it all, you just need to give him a little something, like baiting a hook.

Here are some example bios that generate interest:

I'd describe myself as fun-loving, ambitious and notoriously organised. I think I may also be the only person who hasn't watched Harry Potter. I'm such a foodie – the key to my heart is Italian, so take note ;) On the weekend, I'm usually down at the gym, seeing friends and watching movies (excluding Harry Potter).

According to my 2ⁿᵈ grade report card, I'm an angel (still true today). I love good food, good wine and good times! Last time I cried: Watching that YouTube video of the lion reunited with his trainer (ah man, gets me every time!). Always up for dessert.

I'd say I'm funny, kind, grateful, humble… ok maybe not the last one. Skills include: switching tabs from Facebook to something work-related really fast when my boss approaches. I love old movies, adventure and a good cheese board. If you like all 3, you're probably the one.

Someone once described me as "pretty hot for a ginger" (not sure if that's a compliment). My simple pleasures include fresh sheets, singing in the shower and an empty inbox. I don't want to brag, but I used to be able to do "the worm", kind of.

My friends would say I'm kind, positive, and ambitious. I'm also going to add hilarious. I spend most days building my business, which I love. I believe Sundays are for baking and drinking copious amounts of tea. Additional information: I'm immune to brain freeze. Hit me up!

Not only are these bios fun and interesting, they are also loaded with hooks. They leave the guy with unanswered questions. Often the hardest part is getting the conversation started, so make it easy for him. You want him to be thinking, "I've got so many questions!", not "What do I say?"

Below is a list of bio sentence starters. To create your bio, I want you to pick between three to five sentence starters from the list below, then complete the sentences with something interesting about yourself:

I'd describe myself as …
My friends would say I'm …
My mom would say I'm …
According to my 2ⁿᵈ grade report card I'm …
I'd say I'm …
Someone once described me as …
Improvement points: …
I'm secretly into …
My typical Sunday involves …
We'll get along if …
I'm convinced that …
Someone once told me I'm …
On the weekend I'm …
The way to win me over is …
I'll know I've made it when …
I would love to learn …
I won't shut up about …
I know the best spot in town for …
I have an irrational fear of …
I recently discovered that …
I believe Sundays are for …
I'm overly competitive about …
I spend a lot of time thinking about …
Most people don't know I …

I spend most of my day …
My dream dinner guest would be …
I also …
I have an unusual talent for …
My party trick is …
I am legitimately bad at …
I am ashamed to admit I …
I know my way around …
I don't mean to brag, but …
My greatest strength is …
My go-to karaoke song is …
My greatest skill is …
I always wanted to …
My first CD was …
My simple pleasures include …
My bucket list includes …
Skills include: …
Other information: …
I geek out on …
A life goal of mine is to …
Growing up I …
I'm embarrassed to say I …
Last time I cried: …
Weekends are for …
Secret talent: …
I think I'm the only girl who doesn't like …
I love Sundays spent …
People are surprised that I …
I'm such a …
I think I may be the only person who …
The key to making me laugh is …
I've never experienced …
Believe it or not, I …

I believe in …
I'm very average at …
You'll know I like you if …
The highlight of my day is …
I have to admit, I …
The dorkiest thing about me is …
I get along best with people who …
The key to my heart is …
A whole lot of my life involves …
Fact: I …
This year I really want to …
We'll get along if …
Always up for …
I'm convinced that …
I overuse the word …
I think I'm the only person who …
I have a weakness for …
I've always wanted to …
I love …
Lover of …
I'm the only person who doesn't like …
I've never seen …
I'd rate myself 9/10 in …
One day I would love …

Whichever you choose, ensure that the statements you are making are creative and personal to you. You must elaborate on each point, so no one-word answers. You can use your bio to demonstrate the different sides of your personality. Showing a contrast in your personality brings out the depth of your character, which he will want to see. Don't be tempted to play it safe; being safe is risky in the long run. You want to communicate the things that make you interesting and different.

It's best to start your bio with a short description of yourself such as '*I would describe myself as …*' or '*My friends would say I'm …*' If you're unsure, ask friends and family how they would describe you. Starting with a description sets the bio off nicely, followed by a handful of other statements from the list.

It's imperative that your bio is honest. Don't make anything up for entertainment or pretend to be someone you are not. Lies will catch up with you eventually so don't do it.

Once again, a guy will be attracted to your feminine side, so make sure you bring out your femininity in your bio. A masculine sounding bio will be a turn off because he's looking for a girl-friend, not a buddy.

A little humility and self-deprecation can work a treat too as it helps you appear more approachable and normal. If your profile is too shiny and perfect, you become un-relatable. You don't want to show that you take yourself too seriously. However, too much self-deprecation will put him off. Be subtle in your approach. You want to sell yourself, after all.

Now you have your three to five sentences, I want you to link them together to form your paragraph. Feel free to add variation to ensure your paragraph flows. The finished product should give the guy an insight into your personality and lifestyle, while making him laugh. Random anecdotes and quirks are always good. Remember, you want to be seen as different than all the rest.

Always check your bio for spelling and grammar before you post, as errors can be a turn off. Carefully selected emojis can empha-size your point and make your bio more eye catching, but keep it to no more than a couple. Too many emojis look immature.

Once you've written your bio, put yourself in the guy's shoes. Is your bio presenting you in an honest, fun and engaging way? Are there enough hooks that will encourage him to ask more questions?

SUMMARY

- Your bio serves two purposes—to describe you and to generate conversation
- Be creative with your writing style
- Load your bio with hooks that will make conversation easy
- Set yourself apart from the masses

CHALLENGE:

Write your bio now. It doesn't have to be perfect, just get it up there. Messy action is better than no action. You have time to improve it later.

OTHER FEATURES

Different apps have different features. This can include job title, education, height, religion, what you're looking for, additional interests, music links and social media links.

These are all features you can use to provide more information about yourself. This gives him a greater insight into you and your life and provides more hook points for conversation.

By filling out your profile with all the additional information, it demonstrates that you're serious about using the platform. An incomplete profile signals that the person using the platform is not serious. A man wants to see that you are committed and not a flake.

When completing the additional features on the platform, make sure it paints you in a positive light. Providing boring and predictable information will turn a man off, so keep it fun, interesting and unique to you. Be honest about the information you're providing and don't be tempted to lie or bend the truth as you will get found out sooner or later. When adding additional features, always see it from his perspective. Does the information you've provided improve your bio?

If there is the option to share your social media, I'd recommend you do it. You want to be transparent so he can look you up and see that you are a real person. Furthermore, allowing him to peruse your social media allows him to become more invested. Believe me, if he likes you, he'll be staring at your photos all day.

SUMMARY

- Use additional features to provide more information and hook points
- Make sure these add value to your profile

YOUR ONLINE PRESENCE

Your online presence is the trace you leave on sites and apps outside of the dating app. This may include websites, blogs and social media profiles such as Instagram, Facebook, Twitter, and LinkedIn.

This area often gets forgotten. It's not just your dating profile he'll be looking at. If a man is considering going on a date with you, he will very likely check you out elsewhere online.

There are two reasons for his investigation. Firstly, he wants to learn more about you, what you're like and how you live your life. Secondly, he wants to know that you are who you say you are.

Having your online presence in tip top condition will be a huge benefit. When he does his research, and finds your social media profiles, containing photos and information of you living your best life, he will feel comfortable and excited to meet you. Your online presence outside of your dating profile can do most of the work for you.

Nowadays, everyone searches one another online, and I guarantee he will be looking you up too. You want him to be able to find you easily so he can learn more about you and feel confident that you are the person he's engaging with on the app. For him to find you online, you need to make it easy for him. By providing social media links in your profile, he will be able to quickly find your surname and look you up.

Make sure that your online presence, including all your social media profiles, represent you well. This means uploading high quality content, including great photographs and written content. It's essential that your online presence must be congruent with your dating profile. You want to see this as an extension of the image you're putting forth.

It is advisable to leave your social media profiles public or partially open to allow him to have a dig. This way he can see your content and how you interact with your network. Having an open online presence builds trust as it shows that you are an open book and have nothing to hide. Furthermore, keeping an open profile removes resistance and lets him invest in you. By having the same photos on both your dating profile and your social media, it gives him the reassurance that you are who you say you are.

From my own personal experience, I once matched with a girl whose profile was great. She was attractive and her conversation was good. However, before I asked her out, I decided to look her up on Google. It was there I came across her Twitter feed which contained pages and pages of complaining, negativity and man-hating. I was surprised and disappointed because I liked her, but I decided that I didn't want to take it any further as I knew we had a different outlook on life.

Ensure that your presence online is well presented and respectable. Remove any posts, photos, videos, comments or blog posts that may be detrimental to your public image. This includes any content containing reference to previous relationships. A tidy social media feed is always best. If your feed looks messy, have a clean-up. You can test what he will see by searching your own name on another person's phone or computer to see what appears.

As a side note, not all guys will come through the dating app. In fact, many guys may message you through your social media platforms. If this happens, you can stick to the same principals we will be covering in the following chapters for converting your interaction into a date.

SUMMARY

- Make sure your online presence outside of the app is congruent
- Remove any content that will be detrimental

CHALLENGE:

Stalk yourself and see what comes up. Then remove all content which is not favorable.

THE SEARCH

Now that your profile is complete, you're ready to go live. This means you can see single guys and single guys can see you. All apps share the same fundamental process of matching. Matching happens when you show interest in him and he shows interest in you. When you both like one another, you have a match.

Putting your profile out there for thousands of people to see can be uncomfortable at first. You may be worried about what other people think or who might see you online. This is normal, and you'll soon get used to it.

When you hit the public button, your profile will be out there selling you 24 hours a day, seven days a week, even while you're sleeping.

When you go live, you'll be faced with thousands of single guys. Working out who's worth dating can be overwhelming, so I want you to imagine the process like panning for gold—you're filtering through until you find your little nugget. That way you are not going to be swiping 'Yes' to every guy you are only somewhat interested in.

"Never drop
your standards."

The best way to filter through the abundance of guys is to reference the brief that you wrote in previous chapters. This is your guide. You can use this to separate what you want from what you don't want, and rule out anyone who doesn't fit your criteria.

You can also set initial filters within the app to restrict who appears in your search. Filters include distance, age, height, physique, religion, whether he wants kids, whether he smokes etc. By setting your filters in alignment with your brief, the guys who aren't suitable simply won't appear in your search. This takes away a large chunk of mismatches and makes your search more targeted. Setting filters will limit the number of guys in your search, but this is good. We must be selective to find the right guy. Let's say your filters restrict the search from 100% of the guys who are online down to 30%. This is perfect as you know that 70% you've ruled out would never work anyway. Now you can focus on the 30% and cherry pick the best.

With the guys that remain, only show interest in the ones who have potential to meet the brief. Never drop your standards—your brief is there for a reason.

As a side note, fully utilize the distance filter. Relationships can be challenging enough, without the long distance. If you start a long-distance relationship, you're going to struggle. If you're in a well populated area such as a city, you won't have to cast your net wide to find a great guy. Keep your distance filter to the maximum mileage you would be prepared to travel several times a week.

You're going to generate interest from all kind of guys. This includes all the players and creeps, but this doesn't matter. The only thing that matters is the guys that you show interest in. Whether they reciprocate the liking is irrelevant, you don't want to be chasing guys who aren't into you.

You're not going to know everything about him from his profile, but you'll get a good idea. You're looking for potential. Look at his photos and bio. Does his profile align with your brief? If you spot any red flags, eliminate and move on. You don't want to get involved in the wrong type of guy as it will only slow you down. It's better to save your emotional investment for the right one. Your dating success will be largely due to your ability to say no. The better your screening, the more probability of you finding the right guy. Remember, by saying yes to the wrong guy, you'll be saying no to the right guy.

Also, be mindful not to fill in the gaps. His profile will only give you a small glimpse into his life and personality, and may not be a true reflection. We can sometimes see the 5% and make up the other 95%. This is known as the 'halo effect'. If he has great photos or bio, you might assume that everything else about him is great. These assumptions can result in us being led by our emotions and missing the obvious red flags. The key is to stay objective and not make assumptions. A guy needs to prove his value to you through his actions before you make an emotional investment in him.

Be proactive in your search. If a guy shows interest in you, and you show interest in him a week later, he might already be getting serious with someone else. Take time each day to search to ensure your matches happen quickly, you want to strike when the iron's hot. Things move fast online so you must be proactive.

When you do stumble on a good one, like him and move on. Don't fall into the trap of investing too soon. This includes hanging around waiting for him to like you back, or wasting time on his social media. He needs to like you back before you consider making any investment in him. I want you to think with your head and not your heart.

On the apps, there are other ways of showing interest such as winking. Always show interest in a way that will lead to a match, because matches are most likely to lead to conversation. Novelties like winking are a waste of time as they are too passive. You need to convert attraction into an interaction.

Stay persistent with your search. The search doesn't end until you find a guy who's worthy of becoming exclusive with. I can't guarantee you'll find him today, or tomorrow, but if you stay on the path, you'll get the results you're after. Remember, new guys join the platforms every day, so make searching a daily activity.

SUMMARY

- Finding the right guy is like panning for gold
- Set filters to eliminate guys who do not match your brief
- Search based on the criteria in your brief
- Don't make assumptions based on the information you know
- Stay persistent with your search

CHALLENGE:

Set aside 20 minutes every day to search for guys on the app. Like the guys you like, and move on.

THE MATCH

Congratulations, you've now got a match with a good one. I know you're excited, but I want you to take a second and be objective about the situation. Yes, he's shown his interest, as have you, but he's not yet worthy of your emotional investment until he has earnt it. At this stage, we all have a habit of building a full picture of someone based on the small amount of information we have available. We don't know nearly enough about this guy yet to make judgements. This doesn't mean you can't be positive about the conversation that might ensue, but I want you to be realistic—remember it's just a match at this stage.

As you've been selective in your search, I wouldn't expect you to have an abundance of matches, and that's a good thing. We don't want to be distracted with a ton of bad matches, we want good quality matches only.

At this point, take a couple of minutes to do some background checks. If you have access to his full name, go check him out online. Find him on social media, Google him, search him on YouTube. This basic level of investigation will help you vet him before starting conversation. Does his online presence match his profile? Are there any red flags? Check out who he's following. Is he following inspirational world leaders or porn stars? Believe me, you can build a pretty good understanding of someone based on the people and brands they follow. If you're seeing red flags based on his online presence, un-match the guy. It's not worth investing time in someone who's going to cause you issues. Your time is precious and only worthy of those who are serious.

Let's assume this guy passes your investigations. But wait, you get another match. How do you deal with multiple matches? It's ok for you to be matching, messaging and even dating a few guys at once. It's no different than finding a job—you're putting yourself out there, seeing what's available, until you eventually find something worth committing to. There should be no guilt around this. As I mentioned earlier, you are not making emotional investments at this stage. You are simply going through the process of qualifying guys who might make the grade.

The dating cycle from matching, to chatting, to the first date and even second date can sometimes take up to two weeks. If you realize after the second date that you're not really into this guy, you've invested a lot of time and must start again. This is not an efficient use of your time. Continuing your search while managing a few matches at once is acceptable. It's ok to have some overlap at this early stage. Remember, the search only stops when you find someone who equally wants to make it exclusive.

Now it's time for the chat.

SUMMARY

- By sticking to the process, you should only be matching with guys who have potential
- Don't get overexcited or invested too soon
- Do a little background check; if you see red flags, un-match him and move on

THE CHAT

Now that you have a match, the chat can begin. The purpose of this conversation is to get to know more about each other, build rapport, create comfort, and arrange the first date. It's impossible for you both to create a deep emotional connection at this stage. It is purely a preliminary chat whereby you can get to know, like and trust one another to agree a date, with potential for a future relationship to flourish.

This chat also serves as a qualifying round. It allows you both to qualify one another, get acquainted and determine whether a date is even warranted. Not all conversations will convert to dates, and that's ok. A lot of guys would happily skip this step and jump straight to the date, but you're not looking for just any guy. The right guy will want to qualify you too and isn't going to date just anyone.

If you have done a great job of presenting yourself in your profile, he will already be sold on the idea of meeting you, but I want you to use the chat to over-deliver and wow him with your charm and charisma. You want to become his 'hell yes'.

Knowing how to hold down a decent interaction through the app is imperative to getting a date booked. Conversation through a dating app is far from personal, however you can build rapport if you know how. There are many pitfalls that a lot of women fall into during the chat which prevent guys from initiating a date. By being aware of these, you'll remove the resistance and allow good matches to convert into dates with ease.

Conversation must be two-way. This is so simple, but it's amazing how many people don't grasp this concept of question and answer. It's like a game of tennis. Each person must hit the ball back to maintain a rally, and conversation works in the same way. By answering and asking questions, rapport is built with every response. Both parties can learn about one another without it feeling like an interrogation. Every response should contain an answer, followed by a question. If you respond to a guy's question without sending a question back, it's likely you won't get a response, or he will get bored and move on if the one-way responses continue. There's nothing worse than one word answers or no question in return. It shows little investment in the interaction, and this will often be reciprocated in his response. I've been in many interactions online when conversation dies a slow death because my match didn't think to ask questions back. A guy wants to see that you are interested in him too, and not reciprocating with a question about him is impolite. This does not have to feel like an interview. You are simply engaging in conversation that allows you to learn more about one other.

Although it may seem obvious to some, successful conversations online should follow the structure below:

Person 1: Statement. Question?
Person 2: Answer. Question?
Person 1: Answer. Question?
Person 2: Answer. Question?
Person 1: Answer. Question?
Etc.

If he is the one not asking you questions, you have every right to curb him and move on. Good conversation feels balanced. If it feels unbalanced, it's probably not right. You might like what you see, but if the guy's chat sucks, move on. If he has bad chat online, he will likely have bad chat in real life too. You don't have time to be waiting for miracles, move on and find someone who you can connect with.

Asking the right questions is critical. For engaging conversation, you need to ask many open questions as opposed to closed questions. Open questions allow for longer/higher value answers, whereas closed questions allow for short/low value answers, typically where the answer can only be 'yes' or 'no'. Open questions are not always appropriate, but if in doubt, keep it open.

For example, let's imagine his bio says he runs his own business. Closed questions might include 'Where do you work?' or 'How long have you done that for?' These questions will result in short, non-insightful and boring answers that limit the options to ask further questions.

Rather than a closed question, let's assume that instead you asked an open question like 'What made you decide to start your own business?' Due to the nature of the question, he can only respond with a longer, higher value answer which reveals more about himself. He might respond with an answer like 'I wasn't fulfilled in my old job and felt confident I could do it myself, so I took the risk. Now I have my own team and have more freedom to travel and see my family'. An answer like this is filled with jump-off points that help you steer the conversation. In this case, you could ask more open questions about his team, travel and his family. By asking open questions, you will never run out of conversation.

A guy might have superb chat, but if you're asking him closed questions, you're setting him up for failure.

When he asks you a question, you can bait your answer to allow for more questioning. Remember, you want to make it easy for him to ask you questions. For example, let's assume he asks you, "How did you celebrate your birthday?" A standard response would be, "I went out with the girls, it was fun." This doesn't give him much to work with. If, however, you responded with "I had a pretty traumatic karaoke experience," he's going to have a ton of follow-up questions relating to the song you sang, if it featured choreography and whether he can get a performance on the first date.

The key to establishing a connection is to learn more about one another and to build rapport through your communication style. This means that this conversation must be centered around 'you and him'. Any topic of conversation other than 'you and him' is irrelevant and does not contribute in getting to know one another on a deeper level. Many people make the mistake of talking about irrelevant external topics such as TV series', world events or the weather. None of these topics help to build a connection as they are outside of the scope. Save these external topics for when a connection is established.

When he reciprocates with questions, be open. By sharing aspects of yourself, you will encourage him to share about himself. Even at this early stage, you mutually want to be able to share your passions, ambitions and experiences.

You should keep your question light, fun and interesting. Avoid any topics which are too heavy, controversial or dull. This period can be unforgiving and must be handled with care. As no connection is established at this stage, it would be easy for someone to

Appily Ever After – A Woman's Guide to Online Dating

move on without explanation. Therefore, don't ask about topics which might sabotage your chances at this early stage. This may require being somewhat filtered until you know each other better.

Here are topics best avoided at this early stage:

- News
- Politics
- Sex
- Celebrity gossip
- TV shows
- Current affairs
- Religion
- Previous relationships
- Weather
- Serious conversation

When we like someone, we can often behave in a way that makes us less desirable. This comes in the form of being agreeable, bland and serious. When we are with friends, however, we are fun, relaxed, spontaneous and able to hold an opinion. We become filtered around someone we like because we become outcome-focused, too apprehensive to say something that may be misunderstood, so we play it safe. When talking to guys you like, I want you to be aware of your impulse to play it safe, and instead consciously make an impact in your communication.

You want to make the conversation engaging and entertaining. This means avoiding small talk. Small talk is cliché, dull and uninspiring, and will not spike his interest. Small talk takes place between strangers and loose acquaintances. That's not the impression you want to give. You want the conversation to feel as though you already know, like and trust one another.

Boring questions like these must be avoided:

- How are you?
- How was your weekend?
- How's it going?
- What are you up to today?
- How was your day?
- What are you doing tonight?
- Enjoying the weather?
- What do you do for work?
- *Etc.*

These boring and predictable questions get thrown around constantly and do not create an impact. I know it's tempting to get pulled into the small talk trap, but you need to avoid small talk to generate interest, build a connection and get noticed amongst the noise.

To make your presence felt, sprinkle some playfulness into your communication. Being playful helps build rapport, chemistry and familiarity between the two of you. This can be done in several ways.

Take any opportunity to roleplay. Roleplay is fun and involves giving yourself or him a fake persona and playing around in that scenario. For example, if the topic of relationships comes up, you could roleplay that you two are already in a serious relationship. Give your future children ridiculous names, decide parental responsibilities and allocate custody of the dog if you get divorced.

If you can challenge him in any way, take the opportunity. If the topic of his skiing/climbing/clay pigeon shooting hobby comes up, tell him that you've watched a how-to video on YouTube, you're now a pro and will probably destroy him at it. Once the challenge is set, set a wager that further strengthens the connection. This challenge can help lead into arranging your first date.

It's great to be cheeky, but you do not want to be offensive. It must be done with good intentions and related to something trivial. Ask him about what he likes or what he's good at, then give him a little grief. Subtlety is key; keep it light and infrequent as you do not want to offend.

The guy will see your playful side instantly and associate you with fun and adventure. This will create polarity between you and every other woman that messages him the standard chit-chat type questions. Taking this approach will leave him waiting in anticipation for your reply. This also jars him out of his typical pattern of responses and encourages him to reciprocate playfully.

The key is to have an engaging conversation which builds a connection while simultaneously being playful and fun. This is the winning combo. Be creative in your communication and don't go with the bog-standard responses, try to make your conversation funny and intriguing. We typically only communicate like this with people we know, so this will make him feel instantly at ease. This will speed up the time it takes for him to ask you out as he will feel like he already knows you.

The first step is the initial message. Traditional wisdom recommends the guy messages first. Due to the fast pace of online dating, it really doesn't matter. Remember that to match, one person shows interest, and the other follows. So, let's say he liked you in the morning, then you liked him at lunch; the match will happen at the point in which you liked him. Chances are, he probably isn't online when you match, so don't waste time waiting for him to message you first—take the initiative and message him. If he's a good one, he'll likely have other women who are interested. If you don't take the initiative, he may be pulled in by the women who did. He could be in back-to-back meetings all day, so to find a match and a message from a woman he has shown interest in will make his day. Not to mention—men love it when a woman messages first.

The goal is to get a quick message out there which grabs his attention and then see what happens. So, what do you write as a first message? This is where most people get stuck.

The best approach is to send him a personalized message that is no longer than two or three sentences. The key word here is 'personalized'. Most initial messages that people send are bland and predictable. Examples include, 'Hey, how are you?' or 'How's your weekend going?' These generic conversation starters are uninspiring and usually result in an uninspiring response or no response at all. Generic conversation starters aren't personal and could be sent to anyone. This wafer-thin level of investment will make the guy feel that you aren't really interested.

Deep down, we all want to feel special. By showing a guy that you have taken a little time to show interest in him, he will likely reciprocate. Psychologists call this the 'law of reciprocity', whereby an act of kindness towards someone will likely result in the kindness being reciprocated. This is considered by many as the most powerful law of human nature. It's rare to receive a message that is personalized, so this will pique his interest. He will feel important and special as you have taken the time to write something unique, and would feel rude by not responding because he knows that you have invested some time to make an introduction. This may feel like an effort, but a high-quality message is worth the investment and will significantly increase your chances of a response.

If you find yourself in the position of writing the first message, I want you to use those creative writing skills we discussed previously. Writing something that's unique to him, in a way that's fun and interesting will set yourself apart from the masses. His profile will give you an indication of what he's into.

The best way to open a conversation is with a greeting, observation, then a question:

Greeting – *Hey (Name), Hi (Name), Morning (Name), Evening (Name)*
Observation – *I noticed …, I saw …, It's funny that …, I love that you …, I didn't have you down as …, I think you …, Etc.*
Question – *(A question relating to your observation)?*

Here are some examples of conversation starters that will get the conversation going:

Hey Joe. I saw that one of your favorite movies is Titanic. It takes a real man to admit it. What were your thoughts on Titanic 2?

Hi Ryan. I noticed your photo at Burning Man. What's the craziest thing you saw out there?

Morning James. I love that you can play the guitar too. How do you plan on serenading me?

As you'll see in the examples, his name comes first. Always start with his name as it's personal and people love hearing their own name. This is then followed up by an observation to show that you've invested some time, followed by the question which opens the conversation.

It may take a couple of minutes to think of something cheeky and intriguing, but it's worth the investment in time. Enough of those openers to high-quality matches will most likely result in responses, good conversations and dates. You're not looking for perfection, but you want to write something good.

Once the message is sent, don't wait for a response. There's a chance he may never respond. You don't know his situation and you can't control his situation. If he doesn't get back to you, it's fine. It's only taken you a couple of minutes.

If he's the right kind of guy, he will match your level of investment with an equally engaging response. From this point onwards, the conversation can flow. This is the reason why an engaging opening message is so important. The tone of your opener will set the trajectory of the interaction that follows. Remember, boring openers result in boring conversations or no conversation.

When conversation starts, you must be pro-active in your response. From my own personal experience, one positive interaction sticks out. A girl I matched with jumped straight into conversation, no delay. In an instant, we were messaging live without the boring hour delay between responses. I loved her enthusiasm and I knew we would get along when we met the next day.

App dating is fast moving and you cannot wait around. With the number of messages flying around online, it's easy for your message to be pushed back and forgotten. Furthermore, delaying only kills the momentum and excitement of the conversation.

If you delay, it is likely that your match will mirror your low interest and the interaction will fizzle. You must be quick and consistent with your responses to show you are reliable and interested. Try to start conversation or respond within an hour. If he takes a while to get back to you, don't play the 'he took two hours, so I'll take 2 hours' approach. As I said, you must strike while the iron is hot. This is because it's often the most familiar matches that convert into dates. If you are genuinely busy, for example you work during the day, let him know that you're working and you'll message him back when you can. He'll appreciate your honesty and transparency.

In my experience, I've found that the matches who have been most engaged socially at this early stage are typically the most engaged when the date happens. By making conversation easy and entertaining at this stage, it gives him confidence that the date will be equally fun, stimulating and exciting. I have found that the best conversations are those when both are leaning in, asking engaging questions and wanting to learn more about each other.

Although I recommend responding quickly, I want you to take the time to write quality messages. Not only does the content need to help build rapport, it must be grammatically correct. Take time to read each response to ensure they make sense and are free of spelling mistakes and punctual errors before you press send.

"Finding your dream man is a numbers game."

Unfortunately, not all interactions are going to end well. Some guys just do not know how to behave respectfully. For example:

- He's rude
- He's arrogant
- He asks for photos
- He asks for personal information
- He asks for money
- He turns the conversation sexual
- He asks to meet too early
- He takes a long time to respond without explanation
- He doesn't ask questions
- He doesn't answer your questions
- He's vague in his answers
- You sense he's lying

Most guys are not like this, and the actions of a few idiots aren't indicative of the entire male gender. However, when this does happen, block him and move on without question. This type of guy does not deserve your time.

You're likely to get messages from guys who are nice, but you just aren't that interested in them. You are under no obligation to respond to every message you receive on the app. If you've been speaking for some time and you're not feeling the connection, be kind. Let him know nicely that you're not a fit. You're dealing with people, so treat them with the courtesy you would expect to receive. By letting the wrong ones go, it will give you space for when the right guy comes round.

Sometimes you'll be talking to a guy and suddenly he'll stop responding. Ghosting is unfortunate, especially when you like the guy. There are a ton of reasons why a guy might disappear. He may have met someone else, deleted the app, got back with his ex or just wasn't feeling it. In most cases, he's not interested but doesn't want to upset you. You must accept that in the world of app dating, people vanish sometimes. When this happens, move on. By not getting emotionally invested too soon, you'll avoid upset if he does vanish suddenly.

Now, let's assume you've matched with a guy you like and the interaction is going well. Now you're ready to meet face to face. The right guy who knows what he wants will ask you out. If you feel comfortable, give him your number so you can take the interaction off the app. You should never feel rushed into a date. You should only do so when you feel it's right. This typically comes after rapport is built and you feel you can trust the guy.

You may avoid giving your number because you feel nervous. For any relationship to develop, you must take the interaction offline. If you stall a great interaction, he'll assume you're not interested and move on. When you find yourself making excuses, be brave and make it happen.

You may find that the interaction is going well but he's just not asking you out. Some guys are a little inexperienced and may not know how to pick their moment. You've got to keep in mind that most guys have not been taught courtship and some have been in relationships for so long that they have never dated. You can be subtle, or you can be more direct if he's not getting the hint. You can let him know that it's fine for him to ask you out. You could hint with 'by the way, I'm free on Sunday if you want to hang out', or 'when are you going to ask me out?' I know it's customary for a guy to initiate the date and you probably feel uncomfortable asking, but don't let his oversight ruin something that could be great. Give him a nudge and let him take it from there.

Now that he has your number, you should no longer be communicating on the dating app. By taking this off the app and onto instant messenger like WhatsApp or text, you have both made it to the next stage. You should never go back to the app from this point onwards. Communicating on the dating app is taking a step backwards.

The next step is to arrange the date. Rather than diving straight into the logistics, it's good to continue building the rapport on the new platform of communication. Maintain a casual conversation as you did before. You can always pick up from the conversation you had previously. It's always nice if you remember something he had mentioned, such as 'I hope the meeting with your boss went well today'. This shows that you're paying attention and will demonstrate your investment in him.

Some of my coaching clients ask me whether a phone call is appropriate at this stage. If you both feel comfortable, then do it. However, most people aren't so confident, and a phone call before meeting could be too intense. Some guys are just shy when it comes to meeting women, but it doesn't mean he wouldn't make a great boyfriend. For this reason, messaging is a safe bet. You can always call when you're more comfortable with one another.

After some conversation, he should start making plans with you for the first date. It's his job to make the arrangements. After all, he's the one that asked you out. The right guy will know to take the lead and make it happen. When arranging dates, make it easy for him. Give him a few dates that work for you when he asks.

Make sure those dates are within a week, as you do not want a long awkward period of messaging before the first date. You also don't want to invest too much energy into someone you haven't met yet. If there is no attraction or connection at the date, then you haven't wasted unnecessary time on the wrong guy. If he is the right guy, the longer you leave it until you finally meet up, the more likely he could flake. It's best to get your answer swiftly.

Evening drinks in a casual bar is always the best first date as it is low commitment and allows you to talk to one another comfortably. However, he might have other ideas. If he suggests any ideas that are too intense or do not permit you to talk, then kindly suggest that you go for casual drinks instead. He can always save the dinner, cinema or rock climbing for another day.

Arranging a date is a sign that you're on the right path, but don't burn your bridges with the other guys on the app. You still don't know whether he's the right guy who's worth investing in yet. The deal is not done until the two of you are exclusive, so you should remain active online and arrange more dates. This will help you stay objective and prevent you from over-investing too soon.

DO

- Message first if necessary
- Be open about yourself
- Ask open questions
- Send a question for every response
- Focus the conversation on you and him
- Keep the chat light, fun and interesting
- Respond in good time

- Be flirty and cheeky
- Be creative in your responses
- Use correct grammar and spelling
- Be concise

DO NOT

- Wait for him to start conversation
- Ask closed questions
- Be defensive or rude
- Delay responses
- Engage in small talk
- Send essays
- Rush your responses

THE DATE

The date is set and you're now ready to meet the guy. If in doubt, you can assume that he is interested given that he already knows what you look like and has had the opportunity to talk to you.

You will not fully know the guy at this point, but the first date will give you a good idea of whether you're attracted and whether you could be compatible. Keep a mental note of your brief to see whether he meets the grade. Remember, he will also be screening you on the first date, so you won't be the only one.

First impressions count, so you want to put your best foot forward. This involves doing whatever you can to make sure the date goes well. There is no such thing as the perfect first date, but you can do a lot to help make it a success.

When preparing for a date, the first thing you might think is "What do I wear?" Looking good is important, but I want you to understand that the guy will probably not notice or care as much as you do. Guys notice the whole rather than the individual parts, so don't get too stressed about the minutiae. The right guy will value what's important on a date, like engaging conversation and connection.

If you're dressed well, smell good and your hair looks nice, he'll be happy and appreciate that you made the effort for him. The right guy will also make the effort for you too. Remember, keep your appearance suitable for the activity. What's suitable for an evening bar date is different than a lunchtime coffee date.

Safety is paramount. You will be meeting people who you know little about, so you must be careful. Most people have good intentions, however, you should always be aware. Here are some rules to be mindful about so you stay safe:

- Meet a date somewhere public
- Let a friend or family member know where you're going and who you're with
- Share your location with a friend so they can track your movements
- Keep your personal items with you
- Always keep your drink with you
- Don't give out personal information like your home or work address
- During the date, let your friend or family member know that everything is ok
- If you ever feel uncomfortable, make your exit
- Trust your intuition if something feels untoward
- If you feel like you're in danger, let the waiter, barman, manager or security know

If you commit to a date, don't flake on him. You need to stick to the date set in the calendar and arrive on time. He will appreciate the fact that you do what you say you're going to do. You do not want to build a reputation for being unreliable or late as it shows that you do not value his time or his feelings. The only exception for cancelling, rearranging or being late is if you have a legitimate reason. If you're running late, let him know and apologize. If you need to reschedule, give him notice and a good reason. If you decide that it's not right or you've met someone else, that's fine, but give the guy enough notice and let him down respectfully. Never under any circumstances should you stand someone up—this is soul destroying and embarrassing.

If he is late to meet you, be patient and assume the best. Chances are he was held up for a legitimate reason and will likely explain on arrival. If he leaves you hanging for more than 30 minutes without explanation, move on. A guy who does this doesn't deserve your time and you can be happy knowing that you will never need to deal with someone who messes you around. If he cancels the date or attempts to rearrange, allow him to organise a new date. It's his responsibility to fix it. If he keeps messing you around, move on and find a guy who respects your time.

Your attitude before and during the date will set tone for the experience. Before the date, remember to be objective. By that I mean, see him for who he is, not what you want him to be. Be observant of his words, actions and behaviour. You're screening him to see whether he is the type of guy you would like to be with long term. Do not ignore warning signs in favour of being swept off your feet. This will come back to haunt you. You're not going to know the guy well until you spend a considerable amount of time with him, so you need to be observant. Also, see him as he is, not his potential. Many people can talk themselves up, but talk is cheap. Observe his actions, not just his words, until he has proven that he is the type to deliver on what he says he is going to do. You must be discreet in your approach. If he feels like he's being judged, he's going to run.

It's important to go in with the right expectations. If you've pre-qualified the guy, there is a high chance that you'll get along. However, you might be disappointed if he's not what you expected or the vibe wasn't right between you. Don't put unnecessary pressure on yourself and the situation by going in with the expectation that you'll fall in love and run off into the sunset. Instead, go in with an optimistic attitude and no expectations. This involves lowering your initial investment and allowing for your investment to grow as he proves himself. By being objective throughout the process, you can see the warning signs if they appear.

It's normal to feel nervous before the date. This is the natural surge of adrenaline your body produces to keep you alert, causing the butterflies sensation. It's a sign that you care and that you're moving in the right direction. Meeting someone new and feeling under the spotlight can be a little daunting. If you feel the fear is abnormally high, it may be because you are too invested too soon. If you're thinking that he could be 'the one', there's no surprise that you feel the pressure to make it work. By taking an inquisitive approach, you'll reduce that fear. You are on the date to learn about him just as much as he is there to learn about you. The date may be great, or it may not. It doesn't matter. Yes, you want to bring your best self forward, but don't try to force it to work. By lowering your expectations, it will make you feel more relaxed about the interaction because you are not outcome dependant.

Be conscious of bringing an energy that's fun, light and positive. Having the right attitude will make the experience enjoyable and easy. He won't remember everything you said, but he will remember the way you made him feel. Leave him with a positive feeling and he'll be much more inclined to lock in future dates.

So, the time has arrived. You've been preparing for hours, you've been stressing over your hair and outfit, obsessively wondering how your date will turn out. You're at the spot, excited to meet him. What do you do when you finally see him? I recommend giving him a big smile as you approach, followed by a kiss on the cheek. First impressions count, and this shows him that you are friendly and open.

Whatever location you choose, it's important to sit yourself somewhere comfortable and quiet enough to hold a conversation. The objective is to get to know one another as you do not want your environment to be a problem. If it's a bar, I recommend you find a booth away from the crowds and music.

Not only do you need to be present physically, you must also be present mentally. Therefore, do not turn up drunk or hung-over. While at the date, it's critical that you keep your drinking to a minimum. You're there to build a connection and see if there's potential. You are not there to get hammered. Too much drinking will ruin the experience and you'll look back in regret having forgotten the interaction. If you do drink, set yourself a two-drink maximum, one just one drink if you're a lightweight.

The guy will typically offer to buy the first drinks. Let him pay, a man likes to feel as though he's looking after you. For the second round, always offer. He will likely decline your offer but it shows to him that you are generous and willing to contribute. When in a relationship, most things are split. Therefore, showing him that you are willing to contribute at this early stage will demonstrate that you are a team player. After you've hit your one to two drink limit, switch to soft drinks or water.

The most important part of the date is the conversation. If you like the guy, you'll want to build an emotional connection, and this connection only happens through good conversation.

As discussed in previous chapters, the foundation of a great conversation is engaging questions and compelling answers. This doesn't mean the conversation must be structured, rigid or boring. It can still be fun and engaging while having a flow of information that allows you to both build a deeper understanding and demonstrates your investment in one another.

Meaningful conversation is what gives depth to a relationship. This is because you are communicating with someone's true self, not the surface level version that they present to people they do not know. Fortunately, it's much easier and more appropriate to have a deeper conversation face-to-face than it is over the app or on instant messenger.

The trap that many people fall into is keeping to surface-level chit-chat that never penetrates deeper. They then come away feeling that there wasn't really a connection or chemistry. The truth is, you will never know if you are truly compatible with a guy unless you communicate with him on a level which reveals his character.

Everyone wants to be understood, but few take the time to under-stand one another. Therefore, take the time in your conversation to ask him questions that allow him to express himself, his values, his beliefs and all the things that are important to him. That way you get to learn about who he is as a person, you build a deeper connection and he will leave feeling amazing that someone has taken the time to listen. People feel good around those who show an interest in them, and by showing interest you will increase the chances of him wanting to see you again.

Here are areas of conversation that will allow him to express himself:

- His interests
- His passions
- His aspirations
- His bucket list
- His hobbies
- His family
- His friends
- His pets
- His community
- His work
- His home
- His upbringing
- His education
- His travelling
- His happiest memories

By asking questions in these areas, you'll soon learn what interests him most as he will steer the conversation in the direction of the areas that he's most passionate about. It's important to keep the questions relevant and not one random question after the next. When he's talking about one area, dig deeper into that topic.

"Get comfortable
being uncomfortable."

On the date, you shouldn't go straight into the deep questions. Simply ask open questions that help him express himself. Getting into deeper conversation should feel like a natural process as you become more comfortable with one another.

You should also reciprocate in your openness when he asks you questions. By being open you build trust, and this will help him to open up further. If at any time, you feel uncomfortable or you sense that he feels uncomfortable, redirect the conversation. Your date is not an interrogation, it's just a chance for you both to get to know one another better.

At this early stage, you want to avoid topics which are heavy, negative or controversial. These topics include, but are not limited to:

- Politics
- Exes
- Other guys
- Health issues
- Childhood trauma
- Inequality
- Depressing stories
- War
- Sex
- Drama
- Gossip
- How awful men are

It's critical that you listen. Listening is by far the most rare, valuable and underrated social skill someone can possess, and by having this skill, you will become magnetic not only to men, but to everyone. When on a date, this involves absorbing what he is saying and encouraging him to express himself further. By allowing him to talk, you are showing him that you care about what he has to say. However, conversation should never be a one-way street. The right guy will listen just as much as you, as he will want to learn about you, your values, your beliefs and all the things that are important to you.

Here are some listening do's and don'ts whilst on your date:

DO

- Remove distractions
- Be present
- Give him time to talk
- Use body language to show you're engaged
- Ask him open questions that help him express himself further
- Summarize what he's saying to show you understand

DO NOT

- Get distracted by your mobile phone, the TV, other people in the venue
- Interrupt him when he's talking
- Always bring the conversation back to yourself
- Dominate the conversation
- Hijack the conversation
- Argue with him
- Disregard his opinion
- Offer unsolicited advice

You want to bring the same level of playfulness to the conversation as you did during your initial interaction online. When you realise you like him, a common reaction is to start overanalysing and filtering everything you say to not put him off. The result is that you become bland and do not present the true version of yourself, hiding those qualities that drew him to you in the first place. We all do it with people we like, including guys. When we are with our friends, we are naturally funny, relaxed and spontaneous. When we are with someone we like, we can turn boring and predictable. Gone is the fun, spontaneous, challenging and entertaining conversation.

To express ourselves authentically, we must detach ourselves from the outcome. He still has not proved that he is the worth investing in, therefore you do not have to pressure yourself to make it work. You are getting to know him and he is getting to know you. If there's a connection that's great, if there's not, that's fine too. This means that you have full permission to joke around, tease him, challenge him and tell hilarious stories.

If you're into him, you can be a little tactile when you feel comfortable. It may be only subtle at this early stage, but it shows him that you see him as a potential sexual partner, which is a huge compliment for a guy. Men need reassurance to know that they are doing it right. Being tactile lets him feel validated and relaxed in the knowledge that you like him. If you like him but do not have any physical contact throughout the date, he might assume that you are not interested. It's important to subtly indicate how you feel.

Be physical from the start. If you wait too long to be physical, it will feel awkward. Subtlety is key. Give him a kiss on the cheek when you meet him, touch him on the arm when he compliments you, high five him, make up a secret handshake. Keep it friendly and non-sexual at this early stage. It's more natural to have small amounts of physical contact over a long time than a lot of physical contact in a short time. If the date goes well, having small amounts of frequent touching will make a kiss at the end of the night feel natural. But do not over escalate, as too much physical contact at such an early stage might scare him off.

So, what do you do if the date isn't going well? Well it's a high probability that some of your dates will be duds. Dating is a numbers game and you will have to push through the bad dates to get to a good one. If they have clearly lied about something such as their height or age, or they are not the person in their photos, then you have the right to politely end the date immediately. Life is too short to be wasting your time with guys who lie and deceive. Likewise, if you ever feel uncomfortable or in danger, then make a swift exit.

You might find that you like him as a person, but you're just not attracted to him or there is no chemistry between you. In that case, make the best of the situation. It's polite to stay for a drink as he would have made the effort to come and meet you. It's only a short period of time and you might enjoy it.

If your date is going well, which I hope it is, let him know. Guys like to know when they're winning. Tell him you're having a good time, or that you're pleased you got to hang out. If you want to add an extra hour to the date, do it. This will give you more time to deepen your connection. Just make sure you can still get home safely.

You've now come to the end of the date. If you like him, it's good to end with a kiss. Guys are very outcome driven, so for him to get a kiss at the end of the night demonstrates that you like him and he has done well. If he likes you, he will want to kiss you too. If you've built an emotional connection and been tactile with him throughout the night, it shouldn't feel uncomfortable for him to make the move. However, men fear rejection, so most men will veer on the side of caution and only make the move when they feel fully confident that they will not be turned away. You must make it obvious that you're ready to be kissed. Do this by getting close to him, maintain eye contact, hold his hand, tilt your head and soften your voice. At this point he should get the hint that you're ready. When he does kiss you, keep it short and sweet.

If you're not feeling a connection with your date or have no intention of having a second date, don't kiss him as this will only give him false hope. Give him a polite kiss on the cheek and end the date.

I'd strongly recommend not sleeping together on the first date. If a guy likes you, he will want to sleep with you, and would probably be happy sleeping with you on the first date. However, the period between your first interaction and the first time you sleep together is sacred. You want to allow this time for him to become emotionally invested in you. If you sleep together too soon, he will be less invested and more likely to see it as a fling. Delaying sex until a later date will also filter out the guys who aren't serious about a long-term relationship. If he's serious about building a relationship with you, he will be happy to wait until you are both ready.

If he suggests going home together on the first date, tell him politely that you're not ready and you feel it's too soon. This way you're making you boundaries clear without shutting him down completely.

Once you've parted ways, it's good to close the night off with a message. If he's a true gent, he will ask you to message him when you get home safely. When you do respond, thank him for a great night.

DO

- Put in the effort with your appearance
- Dress appropriately for the type of date
- Stay safe
- Go in with no expectations
- Bring a fun, light and positive energy
- Find somewhere comfortable and quiet enough to hold a conversation
- Limit your drinks to one or two
- Offer to buy the second round
- Ask him about things that are important to him
- Be a great listener
- Be playful in your conversation
- Be subtly tactile
- Use body language if you want him to kiss you

DO NOT

- Flake at the last minute
- Be late
- Turn up drunk or hungover
- Make assumptions about him until he has proven himself

- Drink excessively
- Talk about topics that are heavy, negative or controversial
- Sleep together

CHALLENGE:

Aim to go on at least two dates a week until you find your man. Set aside dating time in your mid-week diary where dates take priority.

THE NEXT STEP

After your first date, you're now moving into new territory. If you like the guy based on the first date, you want it to progress into other dates and potentially a relationship. This chapter is out of the scope of this book, but I wanted to give you some things to look for as you move into the next stage.

You might find that after the first date, you're just not feeling it. That's ok—it's all part of the process. You may need to go through a lot of dates to get your dream guy. The key is to only settle when you find an amazing partner and relationship. Remember, if it's not a 'Hell yes', it's a 'Hell no'.

If you need to let him down, let him down respectfully and gently. You certainly don't want to drag it out if you know it's not right. Let him go and allow him to move on too. A simple message like:

'Hey (*name*), I had a lot of fun last night and you are a wonderful guy, but I don't feel the spark between us. I know you'll meet someone great. Good luck.'

'Hi (*name*), I think you're an amazing guy and deserve to be with someone great, I just don't think that I'm that one.'

Hey (*name*), thanks again for last night. It was great meeting you. You're a great guy but I just didn't feel the chemistry between us. I hope you find someone amazing.'

If you haven't made any commitments and haven't slept with him, you've done nothing wrong ending it. If he tries to change your mind, simply don't respond and move on. You've done the respectful thing and made it clear you're not interested.

There's also a possibility that he might end it after the first date. This may be upsetting, especially if you like the guy, but believe me, it's for the best. You don't want to be with someone who's not into you. If he does end it, he will likely take one of two approaches.

The first approach is ending it with a reason, typically via message. Most people feel uncomfortable letting others down as they do not want to offend. It takes courage for someone to break it off, so it's polite to be thankful for letting you know. He may give a reason, but I wouldn't take it as the full truth. We don't want to offend, therefore, most guys will give a watered down or different version of the truth. This doesn't mean you need to know the truth or try to find out, simply accept his choice and move on.

The second approach is ending contact without any reason. This can range from a slow phase-out to complete ghosting. This can be extremely frustrating as you may think things are going well, then suddenly his responses become intermittent or he disappears completely. Unfortunately, you're not going to know the reason why he suddenly vanished. To assume that it's because he doesn't fancy you is unlikely, because he wouldn't have gone on a date with you if he didn't. It's more likely that he's just didn't feel the sexual or emotional connection when you were together. It may even be down to external factors, like he's decided to see someone else or he's getting back with his ex. If you declined him sex on the first date, this might be a reason, in which case you've dodged a bullet.

With either outcome, you're never truly going to know the reason why he ended it, and even he might not know. I want you to understand that this is not a rejection, but is just a part of the selection process. You will be doing your fair share of selecting too, so expect it to come your way. Please don't take it personally. The qualities you possess will be right for the right guy, and he will appreciate all that you have to offer.

A big mistake a lot of women make is going on a small handful of dates and getting hung up on one guy who is not showing the same amount of interest. Having the expectation that you only need to go on a few dates and that nobody will ever let you down is delusional. Remember, dating is a numbers game. You need to think in bigger numbers and expect a fair few let downs along the way. When it does happen, it's a sign that you're moving in the right direction. Keep your head up high and move on. If someone decides to end it, go back to your value list and contemplate all the reasons why you would make an exceptional partner for someone else.

If the first date went well and you are still talking, he will likely initiate date two. This is a good sign, but do not get your hopes up. It is still in the early days and you are still getting to know one another. By date two, you will be more comfortable with one another, so a more adventurous date might be more fitting, although evening drinks still work. The important thing is that you still have adequate time to talk and build connection. Any dates that do not involve talking, such as the cinema, should be avoided until you are firmly in a relationship.

"If it's not
a hell yes,
it's a hell no."

You may have been on a date or a few dates with this one guy and you're feeling hopeful. It's very natural to get excited. You may wonder whether he is the one and how things would be if you were together. At this early stage, you are still getting to know one another and figuring out whether you're compatible. As the investment is low, it can break down quickly. You might have second thoughts and so might he. However, do not burn your bridges with other guys until the two of you are both exclusive to one another. It's not a done deal yet, so you must keep your options open. It's not advisable however to openly tell him you're also dating other people, as he might assume this means you're not interested in him and move on.

You may hate the idea of using the app or dating when you have a perfectly great guy in front of you, but you don't yet know if this guy is really all that perfect, if he's suddenly going to disappear or whether he is willing to make the commitment to you. Don't delete the app too soon as you will set yourself up for more disappointment if it doesn't work out. You also cannot waste time if he isn't going to get serious about you. When he's ready to become exclusive you can both delete the app together.

If you haven't had the exclusive chat yet, he may still be dating other women too. Unfortunately, this is a very grey area and there is no hard and fast rule. If it's a 'hell yes' from you both, it's unlikely either of you will be interested in dating others. But not all relationships start that way, some can take time.

You must understand that there is a difference between the way men and women think about the progress of a relationship. Most women think in terms of milestones and measure the success of the relationship on which milestones have been met—for example, first date, second date, third date, sex, being exclusive, meeting his friends, meeting his family, being in a relationship, telling you he loves you, moving in, engagement, marriage, babies, etc. Men however do not think like that, they tend to go with the flow, enjoying the process and only slowing down if they feel their needs aren't being met. Therefore, do not expect him to be putting such high importance on these milestones.

There is not a correct chronological order for sex, becoming exclusive and getting into a relationship, but here are some guidelines which will help you navigate through.

You might be wondering about when is the right time to hook up? Sex, should not be given too soon. As mentioned earlier, you want him to invest in you before you sleep together. If you have sex too soon, he will feel less invested and might see it as a casual thing. When sex becomes the focus, it will be more of a challenge for you to develop an emotional connection. You must make it clear that you want commitment and that you are not the type of girl to sleep with anyone. You don't want to give him sex only to find that he doesn't want to progress into a relationship. A relationship is the goal and you do not want something casual.

Three or four dates is a reasonable number before sex. But this can vary hugely. The important thing is that you feel ready and you feel confident that you are both emotionally connected. Making him wait for sex is not what will make him interested or make him stick around. It's the connection you share. A guy can wait three dates and not commit and another guy can sleep with you on the first date and stick around. Time is not the critical factor here, however time is what helps form the emotional connection you share.

From a guy's perspective, he will want to know that the sex is good and that it will be regular thing for him to make the commitment to you. He won't feel excited about entering a relationship where the sex is bad, intermittent or non-existent. Therefore, most guys will want to know that things are good in the bedroom before making a relationship commitment.

Eventually, you'll want to have the discussion about being exclusive. Being exclusive is the stage when you're not quite in a relationship but you've decided not to date anyone else. You might be thinking, "Isn't that the same as a relationship?" Well, not really. A guy needs to sell himself on the idea of being in a relationship, which may take some time. You must understand that guys aren't looking for commitment. They put themselves out there to see what comes up. If you're the woman that meets his needs and makes his life better than when he's single, he will be open to the idea of a committed relationship with you. On your end, you should also only commit when he has the same effect on you. Exclusivity is like the stepping stone from dating to relationship. It's not full commitment, but it's a good start.

Being exclusive usually occurs at the time you have sex. If you have made it clear at an early stage that you are looking for something serious, it would be inappropriate for either of you to be dating other people after sex.

Providing you are both on the same page, deleting the app shouldn't be an issue. Treat it as a celebration of your commitment to one another. Make sure you both delete your profile, not just the app. Leaving a dating profile live while exclusive or in a relationship will likely lead to unnecessary grief later down the line.

Starting a relationship is a big commitment. You are making the commitment to be with that one person for the inevitable future, providing all goes well. By this stage, he should have made a considerable investment in you and the relationship to show that he is worthy of your heart. He must also meet your needs and show that he will commit to meet your needs into the future. A great partner is someone who makes your life that little bit better, and you're together because you want to be together, not because you need to be together.

For a relationship to last, it needs constant nurturing, and this process should never end. Remember, it's the very qualities that attracted him to you that will keep him around. You can't become complacent and neither should he. The nurturing must flow in both directions. A relationship is an exchange of needs, and as soon as one or both parties stops fulfilling the needs of the other, the relationship breaks down. Communication is key. By discussing what you both need in a partner and relationship, you have a better chance of making one another happy. Ensure that you both continue to grow as individuals and as a partnership, continuing to invest in yourselves, each other and the relationship.

SUMMARY

- If you're not feeling it, let him down gently and move on

- If he ends it or ghosts you, move on and don't take it personally

- Dating is a numbers game. Expect that some aren't going to work

- The search doesn't end until you're exclusive with one great guy

- Men don't think in terms of milestones so don't expect him to be putting significance on them
- Make sure you are ready and emotionally connected before having sex
- Becoming exclusive is an easy conversation if you've discussed what you want from the start
- For long-term relationship success, you both need to be meeting each other's needs
- When in a relationship, keep up the high standards and make a commitment to grow individually and as a couple

CONCLUSION

Finding and forming a relationship with your dream man can sometimes feel futile, but it's possible if you know how. Just as with any worthwhile achievement in life, you must build your knowledge and skills, and this is no different for dating, relationships and love.

As the philosopher Voltaire once said, "Don't let the perfect be the enemy of the good." In other words, start now. There will never be a perfect time, there is only now. Time is your biggest asset and you cannot waste it sitting on the sideline. Too many opportunities will pass you by while you're out of the game. Making the first move can be scary, but I want you to go out there with your knees knocking. Being out of your comfort zone is the only place you'll grow. It doesn't matter if it's not perfect, as the important thing is that you start taking the actions necessary to meet your dream man. Commit first, then figure the rest out later.

Dating requires work, and it's not something you can leave to fate. You need to take fate into your own hands. Fortunately, your results will be dependent on your input, and this is something that you can control. You'll find that the harder you work at it, the luckier you'll get. Online dating may be an easy and convenient way to meet your future partner, but it still requires that you gain the knowledge, put in the effort and practice repeatedly.

Be strategic about how you're spending your time. Never waste time on things that are not important and instead focus on the activities that are going to move you closer to your goal. I want you to always be thinking: 'Is this helping me get into a relationship?'

It may take days, weeks or months to find your man. Some get lucky and find their man quickly. However, for most, it requires a little patience. Whatever you do, do not throw in the towel. You must be in the game to win, and quitting is simply not an option. If you give up, finding that special someone will never happen.

You're going to make mistakes and experience frustration and disappointment along the way. It's all part of the process. There will be times when you feel you've made a connection and it can disappear in an instant, so be prepared. Never get too caught up on one guy until you feel confident that he is going to be around for the long term. If it doesn't work out, dust yourself off and move on. To feel the joy of love, you must accept the risk of getting hurt.

You're going to experience the inevitable knock backs and disappointments, and things might not work out as planned. However, what you can control is your outlook. Go in with positivity and optimism as your mindset will dictate your dating success. You will have moments of doubt but you must stay the course and have faith that your dream guy is around the corner looking for you too.

I want you to always keep in mind that to attract the best you must become the best. You want to be changing and striving to improve. That means constantly working on improving all other areas of your life. This includes your health, fitness, finances, career, business, family, friends and hobbies. When you work on these you'll find that your love life will improve exponentially.

The type of guy you want to attract will be growing, not shrinking, and he will want someone who is doing the same. Your relationship will become much stronger as collectively you will be able to grow an epic life together. Remember, extraordinary attracts extraordinary and keeps extraordinary.

Ultimately, you are in control. I want you to make a promise to yourself that you will do whatever it takes to find and form a relationship with a great guy. Make the commitment, put in the work, be patient, keep a positive attitude and invest in your growth. Before you know it, you'll be in a relationship with someone amazing, and you'll thank yourself for putting in the work to make it a reality.

I hope you've enjoyed reading this book as much as I've enjoyed writing it. I wish you all the happiness in the future, and be sure to message me on my Instagram (@benjamindaly) when you find and form a relationship with your dream guy.

If you'd like more information on coaching, courses and events, please visit www.benjamindaly.co. If you have enjoyed this book, please provide a review.

Made in the USA
Las Vegas, NV
22 December 2020

14605566R00079